BRITISH IMPERIALISM & THE PALESTINE CRISIS

CRISIS

Selections from Freedom 1937-1949
with a postscript 1989

FREEDOM PRESS
London
1989

Published by
FREEDOM PRESS
84b Whitechapel High Street
London E1 7QX
1989

Publisher's note

*To simplify the sub-title to this volume all articles were attributed to
Freedom, whereas some appeared in Freedom's predecessors: Spain
& the World (1936-1939) and War Commentary (1939-1945), both
published by Freedom Press and forming part of the Centenary
Series.*

ISBN 0 900384 514

Cover by Rufus Segar

Printed in Great Britain by Aldgate Press, London E1 7QX

CONTENTS

Cartoons on pages 4 and 82 by Philip Sansom

"OH, THOSE IMMORAL TERRORISTS!"

Freedom 10th August 1946   *by Philip Sansom*

Editor's Introduction

The USA has for so long been Israel's paymaster that few people realise Britain's responsibility in what has been happening in Palestine these past 40 years. After all Palestine and much of the Near East was under British rule — spoils of World War I which were not relinquished until after WWII.

To study that past is to realise that Britain's motives, when in 1917 the then Prime Minister, Arthur Balfour, promised the Zionists a homeland in Palestine and when his successors after World War II backed out of that commitment, were neither honourable nor humanitarian. They were determined by purely British interests in the Near East with its rich oil deposits.

Already in 1916 France and Britain had decided on the partition of Turkey in Asia (having assumed they would win the war) with France getting Syria and Britain Mesopotamia with an outlet at Haifa. This carve-up depended on the agreement (which was given) of their ally Czarist Russia which would get Turkish Armenia as its share of the spoils of war. At the same time Zionist representatives put in claims for Palestine as 'a national home', 'the national home' and even as 'a national State' for the Jews. Some members of the Asquith government were in favour others much less enthusiastic. The outcome is summed up by A. J. P. Taylor[1] trenchantly

The British government did not at all welcome the prospect of the French as neighbours next door to the Suez Canal. Zionism was a way of keeping them out. Palestine was chipped out of Syria. It became first an International, then a British trust. On 8 November 1917 the Balfour declaration recognised Palestine as a 'national home' for the Jews. The French who had expressed vague sympathy with Jewish aspirations, discovered that their promised share of the spoils had been reduced by a half.

In fact once the war was over, the British in 1919 grabbed all they could lay hands on, but were especially concerned to maintain a military presence in such strategic areas as the Suez Canal zone, and Mesopotamia (now Iraq), with its rich Mosul oilfields, became a British Mandate. Palestine soon became, as Reginald Reynolds[2] in his brilliant articles reproduced in this volume expressed it, 'another Ulster'. Right from the beginning the Arabs had opposed the idea of a Jewish homeland, though they had lived in peace and profitably with the early non-Zionist settlers. Their fears were not groundless. With funds from World Jewry, especially from the wealthy American Jews, land was being bought up in Palestine and the Arab peasants simply driven off. The rise of Hitler in the early '30s resulted in an escalation of Jewish immigrants to Palestine.

In 1937 a Royal Commission recommended the partition of Palestine into Arab and Jewish states with a British mandate for Jerusalem and

Bethlehem with a corridor to the sea. But by the following year a partition commission reported partition was impossible. And in May 1939 the British government issued a White Paper, ending Jewish immigration once a further 75,000 had been admitted.

With World War II on the horizon the British government felt much more the urgency to cultivate the Arabs and their oilfields than the Zionists and their 'national home'. It was only in 1947 that the General Assembly of the United Nations approved the partition of Palestine into Jewish and Arab independent States, and on May 16 1948, the day following the ending of the British Mandate in Palestine, the State of Israel came into existence.

The articles in this small volume end with a short third section in the first year of the new State of Israel. The article on Morality in Politics (p. 92) points to a future which in fact describes Zionist expansionism over these past 40 years. It is surely significant that these new Imperialists have actually retained the laws used by the British in the '30s for ordering deportations of militant Palestinians! The horrors authorised and even encouraged by the various governments (whether Right or Left, Likud or Labour), armed and subsidised by USA governments, from 1948-1983 have been thoroughly researched in Naom Chomsky's *The Fateful Triangle. Israel, the United States and the Palestinians* and one can hardly believe or accept that a people, many of whom have had first hand experience of Nazi concentration camps, who have lost close relatives in the holocaust, even in the displaced persons camps after the war, can have learned *nothing* from the inhumanity of man to man during those war years when as well as the 6 million victims of the gas chambers some 50 million human beings lost their lives, perhaps as many civilians as military personnel.

The 40 years of the State of Israel is a catalogue of brutality and cruelty to the Arabs. The insensitivity of some of the settlers in the occupied territories was revealed recently when they proposed that all Arabs should wear badges stating that they were 'foreign workers'. Soon they will be calling for all Arabs to be tattooed with a number, for there is no question that the Hawks are in control. Since 1967 the Israelis have been in occupation of the Gaza Strip and the West Bank where there are now some 70,000 settlers armed to the teeth and determined in the long term to drive out all the Arabs. Their militancy is almost embarrassing even for Prime Minister, and ex-terrorist, Shamir, who nevertheless only recently declared that 'not one inch' of the occupied territories would be ceded to the Palestinians. In any case Israel has a vital interest in the West Bank which now supplies about a third of Israel's water supplies. Chomsky quotes an Israeli expert as saying that there "is no solution in sight for the water deficiency problems from the natural water sources of the area" if Israel is cut off from the West Bank.

Israeli confidence in its military power and unstinting, unquestioning support military and financial from the USA and the Diaspora, as well as in the submissiveness of the Palestinians has in the past two years been shattered. The Americans don't think they are getting value for their money, nor is the Jewish lobby so sure about the mood of the Palestinians. If they have the slightest intelligence surely events in South Africa must be alerting them to possible future developments in Israel. After years of passive, defeatist acceptance of the occupation a new generation of Palestinians is offering real resistance every day to the new Master Race. And in spite of arresting and detaining thousands without trial, deporting others, burning down houses in villages offering resistance, and killing and maiming indiscriminately stone-throwing and non-stone-throwing Palestinians in their way, the Israeli forces are acting in exactly the same way as the British did during their occupation. On page 40 are listed the Victims of British Rule. It has proved impossible to obtain such detailed official figures for the Victims of Israeli Rule. Instead one has been obliged to fill the last ten pages (94-104) with book references for the massacres of 1982 in the Lebanon and Press clippings for the 18 months of the *intifada*.

The Zionist leaders in Palestine are now old and tired. Sharon, the butcher of Lebanon, and Shamir, the former Irgun terrorist, are loud mouthed politicians, but without massive support from people prepared to spend a lifetime fighting the 'enemy' for a 'Greater Israel' their threats will prove to be just hot air. The recent kidnapping in Lebanon and a whole number of daring exploits over the past years which have earned the 'respect' of some sections of the media here, if anything reveal how desperate is their situation in the long term. 'Greater Israel' requires more 'pioneers', more fanatics. Instead, all the evidence is that more are leaving Israel than coming there. So worried is the government that it tried to persuade the Russians to allow Israeli planes to ferry the growing number of Russian Jews being allowed to emigrate, direct to Israel. At present they are flown to Vienna where the majority prefer a visa to enter the United States than the Israeli 'homeland'! By contrast the new Palestinian resistance is young, fearless, informed and, materially, with nothing to lose and everything to gain' and is proving more than a match for Israeli politicians grown flabby with power (USA guaranteed) and past military successes.

The *intifada* (the 'shakening') limited to its stone-throwing and yes, some home made petrol bombs as well, is proving more than a match for the Israeli army of conscripts and of the settlers as well as creating deep political divisions in Israel. The idea that sheer military strength combined with brutality and terrorism will win in the end was disproved in Algeria. In 1960 de Gaulle was boasting that the French had no intention of abandoning their fellow countrymen-settlers. Had he not sent and maintained "an army of 500,000 men equipped with enormous supplies

. . . and concentrated this very year a thousand milliards of old francs by way of civil and military expenditure". Yet, in spite of being opposed by a people armed with nothing more sophisticated than machine guns throughout the campaign but who were united in their determination to be rid of the master race, a year later de Gaulle saw the writing on the wall and not only were the French forces withdrawn but with them most of the *colons* — and they had been the master race in Algeria for a hundred years.

Time is always on the side of the oppressed. If the Israelis want to live in peace in Palestine they must get out of the occupied territories and take with them the 70,000 settlers or at least the zealots among them. The alternative is the Algerian solution, sooner or later. Sooner if the American paymasters give them the thumbs down à la de Gaulle.

August 1989   V. R.

Footnotes

1. English History 1914-1945 (Oxford 1965)
2. Reginald Reynolds (1905-1958) came from a Quaker family and his activity in pacifist and anti-imperialist movements dated from his encounters with Gandhi in 1930. Author of *The White Sahibs in India*, he was a contributor to many minority journals as well as being an excellent public speaker.
3. Black Rose Books (Montreal 1984). FREEDOM PRESS are European distributors for Black Rose Books.
4. A remarkable article on *The uprising of youth that has shaken attitudes towards Israel* by Bernard Mills appeared in *The Independent* (April 13 1989). The author was director of UN Relief and Works Agency Operations, Gaza from October 1986 to November 1988. Passages from this article are quoted on pages 103-104.

1

Terrorism in Palestine

'Democracy' at Work

The tragic events in Palestine have provided yet another happy hunting ground for Mussolini.

The Press announces that Arab notabilities in Lybia* have sent a message to Mussolini reaffirming their solidarity with the Arabs in Palestine. This message naturally comes as a result of Mussolini's fine words when he called himself the "defender of Islam". On the other hand Alfred Roke, a member of the Arab Higher Committee declared to Arthur Koestler, *News Chronicle* special correspondent, that he was expressing the opinion of the Committee, including the Mufti, when he said, "We know that Italy regards the Arab question only as a card in a bigger game. She aims at annoying Britain until the conquest of Abyssinia is recognised."

However, apart from once more exposing Mussolini as the opportunist par excellence, the events in Palestine show that all Imperialisms, whether they be democratic or totalitarian are ruthless.

Mussolini brought 'civilisation and Christianity' to Abyssinia with bombing aeroplanes and mustard gas. An attempt was made on Graziani's life. It was followed by the wholesale destruction by fire and bombs of human lives and the huts in which the natives lived. The British Government regretted that such methods should be adopted. The British Government also disagreed with Germany's methods of reprisals by shelling Almeria, over the Deutschland incident.

[* Lybia was in 1937 an Italian colony — Editor]

9

And yet the British Government does not deprecate such action on the North West Frontier, or in Palestine.

As a result of the destruction of various aerodromes, General Wavell, Commander in Chief of the British Forces in Palestine ordered the destruction of houses belonging to "Arab extremists, suspected of having been involved in these acts of incendiarism".

Le Temps reports that an order from Jerusalem states that "amongst the punitive measures taken by the authorities in order to put an end to the wave of terrorism which has broken out in the country, the houses in regions where arms have been stolen are to be 'branded' in equal numbers to the number of arms stolen. For one rifle stolen, one house will be blown up, for one rifle handed back one house will be exempted.

By order of the authorities and to repress the last acts of terrorism, twenty houses were dynamited today in different villages suspected of having sheltered rebels."

Further, *Le Temps* (October 20) quotes a telegram from Jerusalem that "as reprisals against the attacks launched by Arabs in Damaria, on Monday, where members of the police force were obliged to give up their arms and ammunition, a detachment of British troops, aided by police authorities, the following morning dynamited three houses in the town". It should be noted that the police had only been obliged to give up their arms and were not killed by the Arabs. So that this incident should not be repeated, the British mercenaries blew up three houses. And the National Press talks of Democracy! And British Ministers talk of the 'ruthless' tactics of Mussolini and the 'Reds' in Spain!

27th October 1937   R

Facts Concerning Palestine

To the Editor of *Spain and the World*.

Dear Comrade,
Allow me to inform the readers of your worthy paper of a few facts concerning Palestine.

I did not do this till now, for I was under the impression that your paper was dedicated only to Spain, however the article, 'Terrorism in Palestine', which appeared in No. 22 of your paper (27th October) convinced me that you are also interested in 'the World'.

Just a few figures from August, 1936, to the end of that year. The Arabs in Palestine killed about 130 Jews and wounded about 400. The number of attacks on the Jewish colonies and on the Socialistic Commonwealths reached two thousand. Two hundred thousand fruit trees were uprooted, and one hundred and seventy thousand dunam (42,500 acres) of wheat fields were consumed by fire. We must also add that the destroyed property belonged mostly to the Socialistic colonies; and that the majority of those killed were workers. (The rich can remain in their houses more or less safe, while the worker must leave his home in order to earn his livelihood.) One thousand three hundred and seventy bombs were thrown; a number of them being thrown in busy streets and in the *schools*. This is the trial balance of 1936, and along this same road went 1937, the balance sheet of which has not yet been drawn up. Your article tells only of the destruction of the aerodromes and the peaceful seizure of arms from a detachment of the Palestine Police Force. It is hardly possible that you did not know all that I have mentioned above; and if you did not know, why did you 'shudder' only at the demolition of a few houses?

The homes of whom? Here we come to the main characteristic of the Arab terrorist movement in Palestine. Your correspondent dwells in England, reads *Le Temps* and shudders at learning of the destruction of the houses of the poor peasants. But were he in Palestine and had he visited the Arab country places, he would have been surprised to see how small the number of houses in the Arab villages. The majority of the impoverished farmers live in dilapidated clay huts. The four or five buildings belong to the rich of the village: the 'feudal lords', the effendis. To them belongs also the entire land of the village. They exploit to the nth degree those dwellers in the clay huts.

For generations they lived by this type of exploitation. Then came the Jewish immigration. The effendis saw in this new fields of income.

The Jewish people, thirsting for soil, were willing to pay any price in order to be allowed to work the soil of which they had been deprived for thousands of years. The price of land increased, exorbitant prices were asked, but even under these terms, buyers were found, the result being that the effendis, the legal owners of the lands, became wealthier and wealthier. They built themselves new mansions in their villages, opened new enterprises in the cities, and even in the industries their hand was felt; but they still received a great income from their leased lands.

The Jewish immigration caused a boom in the existing wage scale. More and more Arab farmers turned to the cities where the economic situation was better. Thus they began to awaken and to demand the rights of workers and farmers. Fighting to establish better conditions, they received aid from the collective Jewish workers' organisation — the Histadruth. No wonder that fright filled the hearts of the feudal lords; owners of land, and the bourgeois class.

Let us take into consideration that even today, workers in Egypt are receiving three of four piasters per day's work (five piasters per shilling). Such were the conditions in Palestine before Jewish immigration. Compare this with the minimum daily wage of the Arab worker in Palestine; you will see that he receives from 10 to 15 piasters per day, and gets as much as 18 to 20 piasters in places where he works with Jewish labourers or in Jewish enterprises; or in places which have been influenced by the Jewish industrial unions. Now it is possible to understand the panic of the Arab ruling classes and their hatred of the Jews and Jewish projects.

The same Moslem Council (whose Chairman, the Mufti, is also Chairman of the Arab High Commission) which pretends to protect the Arab masses in Palestine, published just a month ago a proclamation to the Arab nation, stressing that the weekly day of rest is against the religious teachings of their belief, and so it is prohibited to all faithful followers to demand this day of rest. Is it known to the readers of your paper that now (with the exception of Arabs working with Jews or in Jewish enterprises) there is no day of rest for the Arab workers?

He who wishes to seek the true crimes of the British

Government in Palestine must know how it caused the failure of the unity of Jewish and Arab workers and their united industrial strife. He should know how the police force during the famous Arab 'strike' arrested Arab workers who distributed proclamations of peace with the Jews and against the 'strike', which was led by the blackest exploiters.

As for the 'peaceful' seizure of arms from the police near Damaria, your correspondent waxes indignant only on account of the destruction of three of the houses in the village. I wish to state that by these very same arms a few days later a Jewish worker was killed while returning from work in the neighbourhood of the village. By the hands of these people, Jewish workers are killed almost daily, for the only crime of not being born Englishmen, Frenchmen or Arabs, but that they are the sons of a nation deprived of a homeland, are the victims of all scoundrels and reactionaries!

And what was this strike? How was it started? By the aid of paid terrorists, who terrorised the Arab masses, within full view of the Government and without its intervention. This terrorism did not even hesitate to kill impoverished Arab farmers who brought their products to the cities to be sold.

But there were persons and institutions who did not feel the hand of the terrorists. These were the Arab banks (they were open during the entire strike) which did not forget to demand the prompt payment of loans. These were also the same wealthy class that subscribed to the riots and the rioters, but did not withdraw their demands of rentals from those Arab farmers, who in order to pay them, had to bring their products to the cities, and because of this strike-breaking were assassinated by the protectors of the 'General Strike'.

And how did the strike end? Plain and simple! The harvesting of citrus fruit drew near (the citrus groves, after feudal taxes, were the largest means of income to the bourgeois class), and their owners could not very well give up their profits. On their demands the strike was stopped.

And the Jews? They also are not stainless, for they, as all large movements (and the Jewish colonisation movement is a mass movement) were not free from mistakes. However, in their internal relationship, and also in their relationships with the Arabs, their sins pale in the light of the aims of the Arabs against the Jews and of the Arab ruling class against their own people.

It is understood that also amongst the Jews the hands of

property are not clean. There is a known number of wealthy persons and of reactionary classes that endorse small groups of chauvinistic nationalists, who are identified with European Fascism, and if you heard lately about the acts of vengeance on Arabs by Jews, know that these acts were perpetrated by the above-mentioned groups (here is not the place to narrate all the incidents of their 'working from within', such as the breaking of strikes, and the assassination of the workers' leader, Chaim Arlossorof in 1933). It is interesting to note that from the Arabs not one word of protest was heard against these groups, nor even against their supporters, the Jewish propertied class. On the contrary, the Arab nationalists are not opposed to the immigration of wealthy Jews; their anger and wrath is turned chiefly against the workers' immigration, against those people who demand their right to cultivate the desolate and the uninhabitable wastes, and the right to work for Jewish employers, for whom the workers' immigration created, as for themselves, a special atmosphere of independence and self-respect, which draws to this forsaken corner of Asia thousands of Jews whose lives had been turned into a hell in the 'civilised' countries of Germany, Poland, Roumania, etc. They, the workers, are the first victims of criminal incitement and they also stand guard on three fronts: against the colonial administration, the Arab terrorists, and the Jewish Fascists, who are now beginning to raise their heads.

For a long time the Government watched from the sidelines all that took place, in her exploitation of race and class hatred for her own aims. **Divide et Impera!** until there entered into the struggle a third power, German and Italian Fascism. Then England herself took over the reins, though the **Divide** succeeded 100 per cent, the **Impera** was in danger.

But, as we sow, so shall we reap. It is now imposs'ble to change that which was prepared during the course of many years. The Palestinian administration did not wish to, and could not, keep control of the situation. Only now is it attempting to do by force, what previously could have been done by non-support alone. It is no wonder that in attempting to protect her own interests she sometimes finds the means to root out the evil at its source. I am referring again to the destruction of the houses of the rich. The Government knows full well what is the prime mover in this unbridled hatred — property — and she is fighting this hatred by destroying the property of those who would sacrifice the lives of human beings for the protection of their property. The fear of the immediate and actual destruction of their property is greater than the fear of some future social change, and the above-mentioned method, therefore, may succeed. But it is almost certain that this method will not benefit now, as the rich Arab villagers are not the principal instigators to date. The principal instigators stood at the head of cities and Government agencies, such as the Moslem Council, and even received Government wages. Only now, after the murder of several Englishmen, did the Government take active measures against these instigators. Several were arrested and exiled; others, the most dangerous, were allowed to escape to Syria and there organise mercenary terrorist groups, which, with the aid of German arms and Italian money, continued their acts of terrorism in Palestine, to which most of the Palestinian Arabs refuse to lend a hand.

What does Alfred Roke state, according to your article? We know that Italy regards the Arab question only as a card in a bigger game! That is how he and his friends regard the matter, but this knowledge does not prevent them from receiving German arms and Italian money, because for their nationalism, Italy and the Jewish question in Palestine is but a card in a bigger game called 'The Fight for the Preservation of the Exploiting Class'. What luck it is for Alfred Roke (who is a Christian Arab) that there are Jews in Palestine, for otherwise he and his co-religionists would take the place of the Jews and fall prey to the hatred of the Moslems, as did the Armenians and the Arab Christians in Syria and Lebanon in 1918 and in 1936, after the Palestinian riots, and those minority tribes in Alexandretta. For, as is known to all, property does not purify, it has always been stained with the blood of its opponents. And how many of them have fallen since Capitalism used Nationalism as a means to divert into a different channel the wrath of those who are forever exploited and swindled!

And we, the Libertarians, which side must we take in this struggle? The side of Arab and Italian Fascism against British Imperialism, or shall we be against the three of them together?

In order to complete this picture of tragic Palestine and to fit it in with the purpose of your paper, I present a few passages from the Arab Press regarding the Civil War in Spain. The following is a passage written six months ago:

"The Jewish workers sent £2,000 to the aid of the Reds in Spain. That is more evidence that the Jews wish to rule Palestine and to deprive the Arabs of their country".

Can someone explain the logic in these words? And again, during the terrible days of November 1936, when the Fascist Press announced prematurely to the world that Madrid had fallen, the Arab papers wrote: "The Arabs at the gates of Madrid". Thus the poor Moroccans that were sent to kill and be killed by the Spanish Fascists were turned into fighters for the Pan-Islamism of the Palestine Arab.

Now that the ignorance and the reactionary civilisation of all lands and of all generations are knocking at the gates of Madrid, and at the gates of humanity, do we think, we upholders of the real humanitarian culture, the *Libertarian culture*, that we have done enough to instil this culture into our own countries? Did we at least *try* to instil it into the countries of the far and near East?

Palestine, December, 1937.   I. ALMONI

(We appreciate the sincerity of this long letter, though it does not in our opinion detract from our article in No 22. We would welcome comments on I. Almoni's letter.)
21st January/2nd February 1938

The Situation in Palestine

Editor,
Spain and the World.
Dear Comrade,
Owing to my absence from England I have only just received your issue of 2nd February and note your invitation for 'comments' on Almoni's 'Facts Concerning Palestine'.

It seems indeed strange to read in an anarchist paper an article which is in effect a defence of governmental terrorism. Nobody who has ever read the daily papers and the Parliamentary debates can doubt the fact that Palestine has been subjected to a régime comparable to that of Hitler and Mussolini, and that the object of that terror has been to maintain British rule in defiance of the known demand of the Arabs for democratic self-government.

Democracy is to our minds an inadequate demand and we may even doubt the sincerity of those who most loudly demand it. But surely those who have seen fit, in the case of Spain, to side with a democratic government against a fascist dictatorship, will hardly wish in Palestine to support a dictatorial government against the demand for political freedom? The Arab leaders may be even blacker than Almoni paints them; it makes no difference to our attitude to their demands, in so far as those demands are just. Indeed, it is doubly important that we should sponsor those demands — firstly, to call the bluff of the Arab leaders, who will presumably go back on their popular slogans if ever those slogans are given concrete form; and secondly because we can only check the spread of fascist ideas among the Arabs and other colonial peoples by proving that we (the Socialists and anarchists and working-class movements generally) are their true friends.

Already we have seen the tragedy of Spanish Morocco, where the Moors fell for Franco's bribes and promises because they had learnt by bitter experience that 'left-' and '-right' governments in Spain were all alike in their imperialism. Why should they care about a 'democracy' which was not extended to their own country? From the French Empire in North Africa comes similar news of oppression by the Socialist Blum Government, which (in the name of democracy) smashed up socialist and nationalist organisations, shot down workers and claimed that the 'unrest' was due to German and Italian agents. The claim may be half-true: *what of it?* Is it not to be expected that fascists will take advantage of the situation when the working-class becomes the instrument of imperial oppression? And does this fascist opportunism make a cause less just because Fascists pretend to support it?

In Palestine we have had concentration camps and deportations, martial law, imprisonment without trial, destruction not simply of a few isolated houses, but of whole streets of dwellings, and the execution of Arabs for the mere possession of fire-arms. All these things are on record and the special measures by which they were made. legal read like fascist decrees — naturally enough, for our fascist dictators only copied where British Imperialism had shown the way for nearly 200 years.

This is not a justification of Arab anti-Semitism any more than it is a justification of the fascist ideas which have spread among the Arabs since the working-classes of Britain, France and Spain made it clear that 'democracy' was a European product and not for export. But if we want to trace the *cause* of anti-Semitism among the Arabs then we must ask how it came about that Jews and Arabs once lived together peaceably in Spain and other countries and cannot do so to-day in Palestine. The answer is, *because it is* *and has been the avowed intention of the Zionists to make Palestine a Jewish country with the help of British Imperialism and in spite of the wishes of the Arab population of the country.* Such a policy could only be pursued by the dictatorship concealed in the League of Nations 'mandate', and Almoni must be aware that the Arab demand for democratic self-government has been consistently opposed by the Zionist organisations for this reason. Zionism is a policy which can only be fulfilled so long as Britain keeps its bargain, made in the Great War,* to secure the support of Jewish financiers. For strategic reasons it pays the British Empire to adhere to that bargain; and the long arm that strikes down the Indian peasant is to-day upholding in Palestine the interests of its Jewish allies. As for 'our own' interests, they have been repeatedly admitted in Parliament and elsewhere by representatives of the ruling class.

I have tried in this letter to confine myself to the principles at stake and to facts which the ordinary reader can check for himself. One can argue interminably about the crimes of the Government on the Arab terrorists, the economic effects of Jewish immigration, etc. The outstanding points remain: (a) Do we approve of British Imperialism? (b) *If not, can we approve of a policy (Zionism) which depends upon British Imperialism for its success?* and (c) *Do we support the demand for democratic self-government* (reserving the right of course, to demand a great deal more than that — but simply regarding this as a minimum claim) *irrespective of the real or alleged motives of those who sponsor it?* No amount of sympathy with the Jews because of their persecution in Germany and other countries can prevent me from saying 'No' to the first two questions and 'Yes' to the last. The very reasons which make one pro-Jew and anti-Nazi in Germany lead logically to the pro-Arab, anti-Zionist position in Palestine. And those who really wish to combat anti-Semitism ought to realise that Zionism is their worst enemy because it has made the whole Arab world regard the Jews as enemies of the Arab people.

18th March 1938   REGINALD REYNOLDS

[* that is World War I 1914-1918 — Editor]

Palestine and Socialist Policy

1. Reginald Reynolds

On June 19th, 1936, a debate took place in the House of Commons. The subject was Palestine, and Mr. Lloyd George explained the origin of the Mandate in the following words. He was referring to the Balfour Declaration:

"We came to the conclusion, from information received . . . that it was vital we should have the sympathies of the Jewish community . . . They were helpful in America and in Russia, which at that moment was just walking out and leaving us alone."

In plain words, a pact was formed during the War between British imperialism and Jewish nationalism, of which the Arabs were to be the victims. Mr. Lloyd George denied this in his speech by vague references to the fact that our troops were at that time "fighting for Arab emancipation against the Turk". How much sincerity is to be found in this statement may be judged best from the observation of Colonel Lawrence in his *Seven Pillars of Wisdom*: "Of course we are fighting for an Allied victory . . . The Arabs would have, in the last resort, to be sacrificed for them".

Sacrificed they were. Lawrence was probably sincere in his desire to see the Arabs freed from the Turk; but in 1919 those who alone knew why the War had been fought were to express their true aims in the Peace. In the debate to which we have already referred, Mr. Amery, a former Colonial Secretary and First Lord of the Admiralty, explained these aims in relation to Palestine:

"In defence Palestine occupies a strategic position of immense importance. It is the Clapham Junction of all the air routes between this country, Africa and Asia. It occupies an immensely important naval position in the new conditions in the Mediterranean."

He then referred to the importance of Haifa in relation to all supplies and the development of an alternative route to the Suez Canal. Others, including Commander Locker-Lampson, reinforced this argument. Their language must surely have shocked those who still believe that mandates are 'sacred truths of civilisation'.

Soon after the War Jewish immigration into Palestine began. It was heavily backed by powerful capitalist interests, which obtained valuable concessions in the Dead Sea. Arab landlords

sold land to the new-comers, but the Arabs as a whole had nothing
to gain and everything to lose. A few peasants found a temporary
market for their produce, while labourers found work in some of
the Jewish enterprises. But in the nature of things they could not
last. 'Buy Jewish goods' and 'Employ Jewish Labour' became
inevitably the slogans of Zionism. The Jewish workers and
'socialists' of whom we hear so much, actually took the lead in this
type of propaganda!

But whatever temporary prosperity may have come to any
section of the Arab community, the net result of Zionism was
plain. The country which had been their home for generations was
to be handed over to a foreign race on the flimsy pretext that it had
belonged to the Jews 2,000 years ago! (It would, indeed, be
amazing to imagine what would happen to the world if this
principle were universally applied. Modern America would be
wiped out and England handed over to the Welsh.) For the
Zionists there has never been any question of settling among the
Arabs and living as equals. They have the intolerable arrogance of
people who regard their own race as 'superior', and the Arabs hate
them for the same reason that the Negro hates the White Man.

Not all Hitler's speeches have done more to create an
anti-Jewish movement than this attitude of the Zionists. In
Palestine the Jews are not a persecuted minority, but the mainstay
of British imperial policy. They know that their position is only
tenable while the foreign ruler remains with his army of
occupation. The Arab demands national independence and a
democratic constitution, but this demand is consistently opposed
by the Jewish organisations. They are the friends of dictatorship
and foreign rule.

To crush the various attempts of the Arabs to revolt, savage
measures of repression have been, and are being, used. Under
emergency legislation, officially promulgated by the Government,
it has been made possible to hang a man for the mere possession of
fire-arms, after trial by a military court. It is hardly necessary to
point out that such a charge is very easily concocted on perjured
evidence. Of its application it may be observed that this measure
has been rigorously applied to Arabs whilst Jewish offences have
been overlooked or leniently dealt with. (Details are given with
dates, etc., in *Punitive Measures in Palestine*, published by the
Arab Centre, 72, Victoria Street, SW1.) Damage to property is
punishable by life imprisonment. The Government holds power to

commandeer any premises or articles it requires, and to demolish without compensation any houses where crimes are supposed to have been committed or abetted, 'the actual offender being unknown'. In Jaffa alone, 600 Arab homes have been blown up under the regulation. 'Collective fines' are imposed on villages 'the inhabitants of which *there is reason to believe* have committed or connived at crimes or acts of lawlessness or violence'. Concentration camps, general searches without warrant, and censorship of posts, telegrams and publications complete the picture.

How this régime — in no respect better than Hitler's — works out in practice, may be gathered from our newspapers to some small extent. Here we can find stories of Arabs shot at sight and on suspicion by gallant Englishmen. But the worst facts are not published, though the authority for them is at least as good as that offered for most fascist atrocity stories. A petition from the villagers of Al Tirah tells of what took place there on 4th June, 1936:

"The soldiers entered the houses, collected what they could of food, clothes and furniture and set it on fire . . . The owners, who watched helplessly, were beaten and struck down with the butts of rifles."

In the end no arms were found, in spite of threats, and the soldiers left having destroyed everything but the money of the villagers, which they took with them. In another village (Al Taibah) 150 men were rounded up and forced to march round all day. Those who became tired were beaten and two who attempted to escape were shot down. One was bludgeoned with a rifle butt as he lay wounded, and both died in hospital. Many similar cases are known of brutality and murder.

Those who know anything about British imperialism will not be surprised at such facts. Imperialism is like fascism — a system of slavery, savage and ruthless when it is at bay. But while such measures have been used against the Arabs, in only one case has a Jew been executed up to the present time. With a few exceptions they are either on the side of the Government or 'plus royale que le roi'. The chief Jewish criticisms of the Government are to the effect that it has not gone *far enough* in its repressive measures!

Our sympathy with the Jews in Germany and many other countries must not blind us, therefore, for one moment, to the reactionary character of Zionism. What is appalling from every point of view is that the leaders of the working-class in Britain are whole-heartedly supporting the 'mandate' with all that it implies. With characteristic hypocrisy, the Labour Party carried *unanimously* at its Conference in 1936 a resolution supporting the Palestine Mandate 'in the interests of the peace of the world'. Their argument was that since 'the situation of Palestine makes it a point of extreme strategic importance and, as such, an object for rival imperialist ambitions' it should remain under British control! But the existence of the Thieves' Kitchen at Geneva enabled these 'internationalists' to cloak the proposal in a suitable phraseology to disguise the crude imperialism of their own policy.

No-one however, has waved the Union Jack with more enthusiasm than Mr McGovern, who in defiance of the declared policy of his party (the Independent Labour Party) has continually insulted the Arabs and demanded even harsher methods of repression against them. When McGovern visited Palestine, the speech which he proposed to broadcast was so arrogant that even the Government, which is too wise to advertise its mailed fist unnecessarily, refused to let him speak. In this undelivered speech (published later in the *New Leader*, with an editorial disclaimer) McGovern produced his Zionist version of the White Man's Burden. The Jew was 'to bring civilisation to the poor Arab' and if the Arab didn't like it 'the law' (i.e. British imperialism) was to operate 'in a just but stern manner'. Whether the people of the country liked it or not, said Mr McGovern, "I say, send into Palestine unlimited numbers of Jews". These Jews were to show the Arab "a higher and nobler life". Most of this speech might be described as pure Melchett, but the final flourish, with its dictatorial "I say" was worthy of Mussolini in his proclamations against 'disaffected' Abyssinians.

More recently, McGovern has treated us to another fascist outburst, this time in Parliament. In *Hansard* of 14th June, 1938, there is a report of a debate on the colonies, when McGovern, having first sneered at the Arabs for being poor and praised the Jews for being well-to-do, tells us that among the Jews young men and women go about in 'shorts', to which fact he adds: "and the minds of the Arab women are being stirred". Now it is not clear as to what particular blessing of civilisation our Roman Catholic authority had in mind, but later on he says that "we ought to be sending the torch of progress into the East to inflame the minds of the Arab population in order to rouse them from their filth". Whatever may be the advantage of Jews and Jewesses in shorts, I can hardly believe that an Arab who reads those words will feel inflamed with anything but a desire to give Mr McGovern a kick in the pants.

McGovern's speech ends with a plain declaration that he supports the Mandate and that he wishes the Colonial Secretary well — strange words for the representative of a party pledged against imperialism! And he hopes that when the present Government goes out of office he will be able to say to the Colonial Secretary: "Well done, thou good and faithful servant". He does not explain how the Colonial Secretary can be the servant of anything but capitalism, or why he should wish to praise him for having served it. That, no doubt, would be too embarrassing, as it would involve explaining why Mr McGovern is himself such a devoted servant of the system which his innocent constituents imagine he is destroying with floods of Parliamentary rhetoric . . .

The problem of Palestine must be faced with courageous realism. The *News Chronicle* (8th July, 1938) in its report on the Evian Conference of Refugees, reports that Colonel White, Australian Minister of Trade and Customs, who presided over one of the Committees, stated that British stock had created the Commonwealth and people from the Home Country should preponderate while British settlers were forthcoming. No socialist or anarchist would, I hope, endorse that view, but there is no proposal that I know of to force Australia to re-consider its attitude by landing an army of occupation and compelling the people of Australia by force to accept an immigration policy to which they are opposed.

The people of Palestine have the same right to determine their own affairs, including matters of immigration, and to decide on policies that we — yes, even Mr McGovern — think bad policies. It may not be too late, even now, to bring the Arab and Jewish people together on the basis of an abandonment of Zionism by the Jews. If so, the first step will have been taken in a process which will drive out first the British imperialist and next the Arab feudal landlords and Jewish capitalists. But unless that step is taken *soon* it will be too late, and the problem, so far as the Jews are concerned, will be to re-settle them in some part of the world where they can live at peace with their neighbours on the basis of a mutual agreement. This does not indicate either Madagascar or East Africa, where the native people have not been consulted and would have the same legitimate grievance as the Arabs.

What is most clear is that the acquiescence of so-called 'socialists' in British imperialism can only drive the Arabs into the arms of the German and Italian agents. They will see in fascism the enemy of the Jew and the socialist; in Germany and Italy they already see the enemies of England. What more is needed but a little more propaganda and financial support to convince the Arab people that the fascists are their best friends? And yet, if this happens, and the Arab world turns to Hitler and Mussolini in the false hope of salvation, the entire fault will lie with British Labour politicians who have shown that 'democracy' to them is a cheap catch-word, to be used when it suits the interests of the British Empire, and laughed at the moment it is used in earnest. All the talk about the Arab leaders being reactionaries or financed by foreign agencies is so much balderdash, because those who use this sort of argument know that it is worthless and insincere. What does it matter who makes a demand or why it is made or who pays the bill if that demand is just? To reject a just demand is to brand ourselves as friends of tyranny and oppression: to accept it and to work for it is not only our duty but the only policy that will expose the pretensions of our enemies. If the Arab leaders are all that McGovern and his friends would have us believe, the best way to show them up is to accept their demands at face value.

29th June 1938   REGINALD REYNOLDS

2. *Emma Goldman's views*

To the Editor,
Spain and the World.

Dear Comrade,
I was interested in the article, 'Palestine and Socialist Policy', by our good friend Reginald Reynolds in *Spain and the World* of July 29th. There is much in it with which I fully agree, but a great deal more which seems to me contradictory for a Socialist and a near-anarchist. Before I point out these inconsistencies, I wish to say that our friend's article lends itself to the impression that he is a rabid anti-Semite. In point of truth, I have been asked by several people how it happens that *Spain and the World* printed such an anti-Semitic article. Their surprise was even greater that Reginald Reynolds should be guilty of such tendency. Knowing the writer I felt quite safe in assuring my Jewish friends that Reginald

Reynolds has not a particle of anti-Semitic feeling in him, although it is quite true that his article unfortunately gives such an impression.

I have no quarrel with our good friend about his charges against the Zionists. In point of fact I have for many years opposed Zionism as the dream of capitalist Jewry the world over for a Jewish State with all its trimmings, such as Government, laws, police, militarism and the rest. In other words, a Jewish State machinery to protect the privileges of the few against the many.

Reginald Reynolds is wrong, however, when he makes it appear that the Zionists were the sole backers of Jewish emigration to Palestine. Perhaps he does not know that the Jewish masses in every country and especially in the United States of America have contributed vast amounts of money for the same purpose. They have given unstintingly out of their earnings in the hope that Palestine may prove an asylum for their brothers, cruelly persecuted in nearly every European country. The fact that there are many non-Zionist communes in Palestine goes to prove that the Jewish workers who have helped the persecuted and hounded Jews have done so not because they are Zionists, but for the reason I have already stated, that they might be left in peace in Palestine to take root and live their own lives.

Comrade Reynolds resents the contention of the Jews that Palestine had been their homeland two thousand years ago. He insists that this is of no importance as against the Arabs who have lived in Palestine for generations. I do not think either claim of great moment, unless one believes in the monopoly of land and the right of Governments in every country to keep out newcomers.

Surely Reginald Reynolds knows that the Arab people have about as much to say who should or should not come into their country as the under-privileged of other lands. In point of fact our friend admits as much when he states that the Arab feudal lords had sold the land to the Jews without the knowledge of the Arab people. This is of course nothing new in our world. The capitalist class everywhere owns, controls and disposes of its wealth to suit itself. The masses, whether Arab, English or any other, have very little to say in the matter.

In claiming the right of the Arabs to keep out Jewish immigration from Palestine, our good friend is guilty of the same breach of Socialism as his comrade, John McGovern. To be sure the latter makes himself the champion of British Imperialism while Reginald Reynolds sponsors the Arab capitalist rights. That is bad enough for a revolutionary socialist. Worse still is the inconsistency in pleading on behalf of land monopoly, to which the Arabs alone should have the right.

Perhaps my revolutionary education has been sadly neglected, but I have been taught that the land should belong to those who till the soil. With all his deep-seated sympathies with the Arabs, our comrade cannot possibly deny that the Jews in Palestine have tilled the soil. Tens of thousands of them, young and deeply devout idealists, have flocked to Palestine, there to till the soil under the most trying pioneer conditions. They have reclaimed wastelands and have turned them into fertile fields and blooming gardens. Now I do not say that therefore the Jews are entitled to more rights than the Arabs, but for an ardent socialist to say that the Jews have no business in Palestine seems to me rather a strange kind of socialism.

Moreover, Reginald Reynolds not only denies the Jews the right of asylum in Palestine, but he also insists that Australia, Madagascar and East Africa would be justified in closing their ports against the Jews. If all these countries are in their right, why not the Nazis in Germany or Austria? In fact, all countries. Unfortunately, our comrade does not suggest a single place where the Jews might find peace and security.

I take it that Reginald Reynolds believes in the right of asylum for political refugees. I am certain he resents the loss of this great principle, once the pride and glory of England, as much as I do. How then, can he reconcile his feelings about political refugees with his denial of asylum to the Jews. I must say I am puzzled.

Our friend waxes very hot about national independence for the Arabs and for all other peoples under British Dominion. I am not opposed to the struggle for it, but I do not see the same blessings in national independence under the capitalist régime. All the advancement claimed for it is like the claims for democracy, a delusion and a snare. One has to point out some of the countries that have achieved national independence. Poland, for instance, the Baltic States or some of the Balkan countries. Far from being progessive in the true sense, they have become Fascist. Political persecution is not less severe than under the Tsar, while anti-Semitism, formerly fostered from on top, has since infested every layer of social life in these countries.

However, since our friend champions national independence, why not be consistent and recognise the right of the Zionists or the Jews at large to national independence? If anything, their precarious condition, the fact that they are nowhere wanted, should entitle them to at least the same consideration that our comrade so earnestly gives to the Arabs.

I know of course that a great many of the Jews can lay no claim to being political refugees. On the contary, most of them have remained indifferent to the persecution of workers, socialists, communists, trade-unionists and anarchists, so long as their own skins were safe. Like the middle-class in Germany and Austria, they have exploited labour and have been antagonistic to any attempt on the part of the masses to better their condition. Some German Jews had the temerity to say that they would not object to driving out the *OstJuden* (Jews coming from Poland and other countries). All that is true, but the fact remains that since Hitler's ascendancy to power all Jews without exception have been subjected to the most fiendish persecution and the most horrible indignities, besides being robbed of all their possessions. It therefore seems rather strange for a Socialist to deny these unfortunate people a chance of taking root in new countries, there to begin a new life.

The last paragraph in 'Palestine and Socialist Policy' caps the climax. The author writes: "What does it matter who makes a demand or why it is made, or who pays the bill if that demand is just? To reject a just demand is to brand ourselves as friends of tyranny and oppression; to accept it and to work for it is not only our duty but the only policy that will expose the pretensions of our enemies."

The question is, dear Reginald Reynolds, who is to decide what is a 'just demand'? Unless one makes oneself guilty of the charge the writer hurls against the Jews, "the intolerable arrogance of people who regard their own race as superior", one cannot very well decide whether the demand of natives for the monopoly of their country is any more just than the desperate need of millions of people who are slowly being exterminated.

In conclusion, I wish to say that my attitude to the whole tragic question is not dictated by my Jewish antecedents. It is motivated by my abhorrence of injustice, and man's inhumanity to man. It is because of this that I have fought all my life for anarchism which alone will do away with the horrors of the capitalist régime and place all races and peoples, including the Jews, on a free and equal basis. Until then I consider it highly inconsistent for socialists and anarchists to discriminate in any shape or form against the Jews.

26th August 1938   EMMA GOLDMAN

3. Reg. Reynolds Replies

To the Editor,
Spain and the World.

Dear Comrade,
As my dear friend Emma Goldman is anxious that I shall not be misunderstood she will appreciate this attempt to set right her own misconceptions regarding my views on Palestine.

I must thank Emma for the assurance given to her friends that I am not anti-Semitic; but I completely disagree with the statement that my article of July 29th "unfortunately gives such an impression". No-one can show me a single sentence in it which, taken in its context, gives any such impression to an unprejudiced mind. Dr. Johnson once said: "Sir, I can give you an argument, but I cannot provide you with an intelligence." I am in the same position, and cannot answer for what prejudice may read into my words. Bakunin was also called anti-Semitic . . .

At no point was my article concerned with Jews as a race or with Arabs as a race. It was concerned with the right of self-government which the Arabs claim and the Zionists oppose. In common with the anarchists I believe that the ideal society is one where there is no government at all. But I also believe that where people do not yet realise this fact, democratic government — that is to say, government by the explicit consent of at least a majority of the people — is better than autocratic or bureaucratic government. The anarchists in Spain seem to be impressed with the same fact, or they would not have given even limited co-operation to the Government against Franco.

But just as anarchists realise that Fascism is worse than 'democratic' capitalism, so most of them will agree with me that imperialism is worse, and for the same reasons. Those who cannot see this as a matter of commonsense, should study and compare conditions — say — in India and the British colonies with conditions among British workers. I do not need Emma Goldman to tell me the limitations of 'democracy' or of national independence; but to regard such objectives simply as 'a delusion and a snare' is to deny the whole basis upon which whatever liberty we possess has been built up, and the present basis of co-operation between anarchists and other anti-fascists in Spain. And for my dear friend to say that she is 'not opposed to the struggle' for national independence is surely a half-hearted gesture towards those who are bearing the brunt of the fight against British Imperialism. As I pointed out in my article, only active support will impress the colonial peoples; and if they receive such support from the Fascist Powers whilst anarchists are content with being 'not opposed to them', I fear that the masses now suffering oppression under the Union Jack may form alarming conclusions as to who are their real friends. *Whose fault will that be?*

Personally I am not prepared to stand aloof from a struggle between oppressor and oppressed because the oppressed have not grasped 100% of the truth as I see it. I shall help the underdog because he is the underdog and because it is the only way of impressing him with my sincerity if I wish to teach him anything in the way of politics or economics. And I shall not be frightened by misrepresentations, intentional or unintentional. I know that to oppose British Imperialism in Palestine (and Zionism, its ally) is to invite the accusation of being anti-Semitic. I know that to criticise the Spanish Government or the French Front Populaire is to brand oneself as a 'Trotsky-Fascist'. Neither prospect disturbs me in the least.

I am not impressed by the fact that Jewish workers have contributed financially to back up Jewish emigration to Palestine. British workers contribute to a number of foolish things, including Sir Walter Citrine's salary. As to the statement that 'the land should belong to those who till the soil', I neither accept it nor see its relevance to Emma Goldman's case. Ideally speaking, the land should 'belong' in my opinion, to the whole community — since all wealth comes out of it. But if I accept Emma's statement, then the land in Palestine should have belonged to the Arab peasant and the Arab landlords had no right to sell it to Jewish immigrants who dispossessed these Arab tenants. That is the only sense I can make out of Emma's statement, unless she means that the land belongs to whoever can grab it — i.e. that it belonged first to the Arab fellaheen but now belongs to those who pushed the Arab off. 'Finding is keeping' is a good motto for conquistadores and imperialists, but not, I should have thought, for anarchists.

Next there are three opinions which Emma attributes to me for which there is not the slightest foundation. I have nowhere 'sponsored the Arab capitalist rights' and I have nowhere said that 'the Jews have no business in Palestine'. Also I did not 'justify' the closing of Australian ports against the Jews. Quite on the contrary. Discussing the views of the Australian representative at the Evian

Conference, I said: "No Socialist or Anarchist would, I hope, endorse that view". Is that justification? But I added that if Australia excluded Jews there would not be an attempt to force her to accept Jewish immigrants by landing an army of occupation. It was simply a statement of fact; but I am prepared to make it one of opinion, and to ask whether Emma Goldman or anyone of her persuasion is prepared to advocate such a step? If I say that I am not going to interfere forcibly with my neighbour's household it does not necessarily mean that I approve of everything he does; and I am sorry if Emma cannot see the distinction.

My attitude to Palestine is based on the same principles. The prime question is not whether I approve of Jewish immigration, but who shall decide on its extent. At present, it is determined by a foreign government — our own — whose decisions are enforced upon an unwilling population at the point of the bayonet. The alternative of Madagascar would present the same problem (though Emma confuses it with the problem of Australia, as though both were self-governing and autonomous). Hence my suggestion that a little constructive thought should be devoted to discovering "some part of the world where they (the Jews) can live at peace with their neighbours by mutual agreement". This is what my dear friend calls "denying these unfortunate people a chance of taking root in new countries".

Emma's worst confusion is in her accusation of inconsistency because I support Arab independence and oppose Jewish nationalism. I support Moorish independence; but that does not mean that I should support the Moors in Spain, where they are the enemies of Spanish independence. I am not, as Emma appears to imagine, interested in nationalism for its own sake, but only where it is an expression of revolt against imperialism. And just as I am opposed to the Moors when they appear as conquerors in a fascist army, so I am opposed to the Jews when they appear as colonists in a British scheme to create an 'Ulster' in Palestine. To follow this Irish analogy a little further, I am anti-Catholic; but in the Irish struggle for Catholic emancipation I should have been an emancipationist: not because I love the Pope, but because I do not believe in depriving a nation of its religion. Just so, in Palestine, I stand for the rights of the people against the claim of a minority to over-ride them, irrespective of all other considerations.

Finally, Emma implies that I am guilty of the same 'intolerable arrogance' with which (she says) I charged the Jews. (I actually used this phrase of the Zionists, but let it pass.) And this because I

have dared to speak of a 'just demand' — referring to the Arab demand for democratic self-government. Well, of course, I may be wrong. Socialism may not be just. Anarchism may not be just. Franco may be a good man, the saviour of Spain, whom (in my 'arrogance') I have condemned. But I'm prepared to risk it; and I notice that Emma too has sufficient arrogance to take sides in a fight when it suits her. For my part I will say that if the cause of self-determination is not a just cause, then the word justice has no longer any meaning for me and can be left out of the discussion. I only know that self-determination is the basic principle of both socialism and anarchism as I understand them, and that I will fight every system of society in which this principle is not fundamental.
16th September 1938   REGINALD REYNOLDS

Two Opinions on Palestine

(We are reproducing these two articles much for the reason that they represent 'other opinions' on Palestine. The fact that we are publishing them does not necessarily signify agreement with either.) — Editor

From the 'Palestine Post', Jerusalem
When we remember the profound influence that Palestine through the Scriptures has had on the religion and the speech and therefore the thought of the British people, it is not surprising to find ourselves carried back beyond historical records to the realm of mythology. In this way the connection between Palestine and Britain dates back further than most people would think.

According to the fervently held belief of some, part of the seafaring tribe of Dan left Palestine for Greece — where they embodied their name in the Dardanelles — whence they made an expedition to Ireland and settled there, even before the days of Jeroboam II. They then crossed to Scotland and were later — fifteen hundred years later — joined by a second part of the same tribe who had wandered in a north-westerly direction overland across Europe and settled in what they made known as Denmark, whence they invaded Britain. The tribe of Simeon became the Scythians, then became modified in name to Kimmerii, then Cymri, by which name the Welsh call themselves even to-day.

They called the country which they finally occupied Britain; they themselves were British, that is Brit-ish, which is Hebrew for 'People of the Covenant'. Now the Saxons are plainly Isaacsons — that is obvious, and the Normans are but a branch of the same group of Northmen. The present inhabitants of the British Isles are therefore simply a re-union of the tribes of Israel, and their to-day's occupation of Palestine — their country of origin — is seen to be natural and pre-ordained.

Thus are first and last things united.

Not only, according to this belief, is the connection between Britain and Palestine a racial one. There is the strongest of personal links. For when Jeremiah went into exile after the destruction of the First Temple he did not go to Babylon, as is commonly supposed, but to his kinsmen in Ireland, taking with him a princess of the House of David. This lady married the ruler of Ireland, who was himself descended from Zarah, the son of Judah, and from them sprang the direct line whose representative in our own day is His Majesty King George VI. So much for mythology, as the British-Israelites read it.

From 'As-Siraat al-Mustakim' (Arab Nationalist), Jerusalem
There has been a great deal in the press of late to the effect that British policy vis-a-vis Palestine is being dictated by World Jewry. What is the truth? How is it possible to believe that a great Imperial power with the resources of Great Britain, and which rules over large tracts of the earth's surface, would humble itself before a handful of Jews; and would be the willing servant of a few million sons of Zion? We do not believe that Great Britain would allow her might and strength to be used in the interests of these people. He would have to be clever indeed who would persuade Britain to take any line of action except in her own interests.

Where is this much vaunted power of Jewry? It was amply proved to the world by Hitler that it was built on foundations of deceit and questionable methods. Thus, we have a man like Dr Weizmann uttering words to this effect to Great Britain:

"We shall remain in Palestine whether it is pleasing to you or not. You are able to accelerate or impede our progress at will. But you would be well advised to render us every assistance; otherwise our powers for construction could well be turned into powers of destruction, which would have disastrous results for the world!"

The Jews, a self-confessed helpless and weak people, threaten the world with destruction! No one should have any fear of these people, particularly now that their weakness has been laid bare by a Hitler!

It is a fact which admits of no argument or contradiction that it is manifestly in the interests of Great Britain to dominate Jewish policy. It is because of this that she favours a kind of Anglo-Zionist policy in Palestine. She is bent on breaking the power — however illusionary this might be — of the Jews as she has of other people who have stood in the way of her imperial ambitions.

Do not the Jews realise that the promise of the establishment of a National Home is rendering their existence in Europe untenable, quite apart from threatening them in Palestine itself? They can never recover their former position in Europe . They know well enough that they are in the hands of Great Britain and that this power is in a position to dictate to them as she has dictated to others.

Let the Jews do some heart-searching, and then they will be compelled to admit to themselves their great blunder. But they lack the courage to give voice to their thoughts for by doing so they would lose the only sympathy left to them: that is, the sympathy of Great Britain.

Looking at the matter from another point, it would be well for all Arabs and Moslems to pay little heed to this mythical power of World Jewry. If the Arabs can convince Great Britain — and they are doing so — that her interests lie in the seeking of Arab friendship, even though the scales are weighed heavily against the Jews, then her policy will take a new turn in the direction of service towards the Arabic and Islamic worlds.

15th October 1938

Palestine — Idealists and Capitalists

The first Jews to settle in Palestine were 'young, intellectual Russians' who left Russia after the pogroms of 1882 'to devote themselves to simple village life'. But the idea of a Jewish State was first envisaged by Theodor Herzl a Viennese journalist. His Zionism had very little idealism about it. As Mr Feiwel remarks* "Zionism was essentially a bourgeois and capitalist movement" and throughout the book, in vain does one seek for any traces of idealism in the movement, save in the only too few Communal Settlements which are generally opposed to Official Zionism. As early as 1920 "in the new Jewish Palestine", the "young and militant Labour Federation already had its ideological difficulties". The difficulties arose because there was, according to the author a "strong Left Wing of young people" with pronouncedly revolutionary views who rejected all bourgeois ties and advocated militant co-operation between the Arab and Jewish workers. Naturally, as in all capitalist countries, the idealist minority succumbs to the wishes of the Capitalists, and in this case to the Zionist Organisation.

This book can leave no illusions as to the true nature of official Zionism. It is Capitalist to the core. In fact, the Socialist dream was shattered as far back as 1924-25. "The brisk capitalist development in Tel Aviv, Haifa and the cities belt took first place" and needless to say there were "bitter struggles against exploitation". And the author admits that though Jewish emigration would continue "it was obvious that the growth of Jewish Palestine under the British regime would be on Capitalist lines and colonial Capitalist lines at that". And Zionism has since abandoned all attempts at setting up a free society in Palestine. Rather has it been the contrary. Capitalist refugees (!) flocked to Palestine while the poor workers who probably had even in some small measure agitated against Fascism were left behind to face the consequences. The author quite expected this to happen when he wrote "Naturally it was the wealthiest and most efficient Jews who had kept their resources sufficiently liquid, who reached the country first". This sudden influx of capital created "revolutionary economic changes in Jewish Palestine". "There was an unprecedented boom in houses, building plots and cities groves,

* in *No Ease in Zion* by T. R. Feiwel (London 1938)

the only ready channels of investment . . ." land value rose to
fantastic heights . . . "and at the same time the Histadrut grew into
a close knit, wealthy body of nearly 100,000 members aiming
entirely at consolidating the new nationalism, cementing the new
Jewish Palestine into a miniature but solid national entity". This
passage is full of irony for most of these 'colonisers' have escaped
from German Nationalism which they have learned to hate by
bitter experience, only to create Jewish Nationalism in Palestine.
There is some truth in the suggestion that many Jews in Germany
would have gladly waved the Swastika if Streicher gave them the
chance to do so! Consequently the Zionist attitude towards the
Arabs is of interest. Nine tenths of Zionist opinion — according to
Mr. Feiwel, considers that "The Arab does not exist", which is not
exactly the best way to try and work in harmony with the people
who have, after all, lived for years in the same land. At least it is
not the attitude one would expect from people who have
themselves been driven out of a country which they had
considered their homeland for generations. And the author shows
us how sure the Zionists always were of their strength and of
outside support. They reasoned in these terms: "Ultimately British
and Zionist interests must surely coincide. And how could a small
Arab population challenge the might of British Imperialism" or as
in another example the Zionist assumption "that such a Zionist
majority (in Palestine) could be obtained without major resistance
by the Arabs, implies that the Palestine Arabs do not exist . . ."
Furthermore one reads "Already the Official Zionist name for
Palestine — Eretz Israel . . . emphasised this attitude". Also the
education of Jewish children in Palestine was nationalist. In fact
the whole attitude of official Zionism has been one of
non-co-operation with the Arabs.

The Arabs and their cause are dealt with in a very sketchy
fashion in a short chapter. The backward conditions of the Arab
worker and his domination by the upper class is surely not a reason
why these people should be exploited and dominated by a Jewish
Capitalist, with the aid of British Imperialism. Nor can one
condemn a movement simply because it has "no programme". The
Arab demand for independence is far from vague in its
significance.

The Arab leaders, writes Mr. Feiwel, show through their
writings and their speeches that "they still only half grasp the real
world" and have besides, most vivid imaginations. That may be
true, but Herzl also had a vivid imagination ("the Jewish bankers

dismissed him casually as a mad visionary") and what of Ben Gurion, reactionary and Zionist who laid down a ten year plan for the immigration of one million Jewish families (that is five million people) and all he required was £250 million!

To be sure there is no idealism in the Arab overlords as there is no idealism in the millions of Alfred Mond "the ruthless chief of Imperial Chemical Industries", but as the author points out, since the war the population "Arabs, Christians, Jews exchanged a decadent Imperial Master for an up-to-date one" and more up-to-date in his ruthlessness. And so long as Jewish immigration to Palestine has as its aim the establishment of a Jewish State where lack of consideration for those outside its circle threatens to shape in a similar fashion to that in other countries, then the Arabs' cry for independence and their demands that Jewish emigration should cease seem fully justified.

Mr. Feiwel, following his detailed analysis which while not favourable to the Arabs is hardly flattering to the Zionists, in the chapter 'Palestine and the Jews' tries to look into the future of Palestine. The narrow outlook of Zionism will prevent progress being made in Palestine, and again — for it cannot be stressed too often — reinforce the lack of consideration for the Arabs who in Palestine "still live at a deplorably low level".

The persecution of the Jews in Europe to-day is in our opinion but one problem, and their treatment is not a greater travesty of justice than Mussolini's murderous attacks on the Abyssinians or on the Italian workers who still fill his gaols, nor of British Imperialism's policy in India, nor of International Fascism's campaign of extermination in Spain.

We say with Mr. Feiwel that "to-day the question of the Jews of Europe has become one which must be solved together with all others — or, together with them, fail to be solved". And we further add that Zionism will not solve the Jewish problems.

The Jewish workers must now unite with the Arab workers, before hatred and suspicion create an unsurmountable barrier, which will make it virtually impossible to rid Palestine of British Imperialism and Arab and Jewish Capitalism, for many years to come.

3rd December 1938   R.

Anarchist Tactic for Palestine

The Arab revolution is centred on Palestine. The re-awakening of the Arab nation and the consequent nationalist revolution has brought the masses of Palestine in conflict with British Imperialism. Every movement against British Imperialism must be welcomed as the rulers of this country rule (or, synonymously, misrule) the larger part of the world's colonial peoples. The opposition of revolutionaries to British Imperialism and its allies must be taken for granted.

The clashing of two nationalisms (Jewish and Arab in this case) has inevitably given rise to controversy abroad. In the Houses of Parliament sympathy is naturally pro-Zionist; as one MP is reputed to have said, when asked why he supported the Jews in Palestine against the Arabs: "In my constituency I have thousands of Jewish voters — I haven't a single Arab". The Labour Party, free from responsibility in the Government of a bloody suppression of all vestiges of Arab life, urges the Government to insist upon the policy of a Jewish National State. The majority opinion here seems to be pro-Zionist, perhaps because the Zionists are so definitely pro-Imperialist while the Arabs are vaguely accused of being pro-Fascist. It would be a surprise, therefore, to read about the Government's rejection of the Jewish side in the Palestine talks (up to the moment of writing) if the Government had not to reckon with millions of other Arab and Moslem subjects in the Empire. Chamberlain's policy of 'Appeasement' has up to now not been primarily in the interests of the Democratic Imperialisms, and in the Palestine issue, again, he is far less concerned with the maintenance of Imperialism than his 'Left' opponents!

What is the case for Zionism? Zionism represents the age-old desire of the rabbis to return to the 'Holy' Land. The significance of the word 'Zion' (the Biblical and traditional name) will be noted. The rabbis, whose jobs depend on the keeping-up of the race-barriers and the consequent survival of the religion, in the fear of assimilation, have fostered these artificial laws in order to maintain, by tribal 'totems and taboos' a separate race. Naturally, they have failed, and Zionism is the way they are endeavouring to succeed. There is to-day no pure race, despite the claims of Hitler and the Rabbis. It will be noted that the revival of Judaism has only been a reaction to pogroms and persecution. In times and countries where there has been complete racial and religious toleration, assimilation has begun; intolerance always defeating its own ends.

Herzl began the move for 'Back to Zion'. Was his primary concern for the refugees, then fleeing from the pogroms of the Tsar? On the contrary, Herzl refused far more suitable land in Africa, insisting on the 'Holy' Land. Finally, the Balfour War Government promised Palestine to the Jews, as well as to the Arabs, when Turkey was defeated. Since the Mandate, the introduction of capitalist Western ideas has undoubtedly benefited the Arab workers, as has the introduction of the proletarian organisations of Europe. *But this is no excuse*, whatever the Zionists may say. Capitalism introduced in this fashion benefited everywhere the working class; the same thing happening in Russia was hailed as a triumph for 'communism'. It was nothing of the sort. Despite the coming of capitalist benefits, the struggle against capitalist malevolences must be fought.

Originally there was no agitation against Jewish immigration; moreover there was never previously any anti-Semitism in the Arab countries. Not until immigration became colonisation, and the aim of a Jewish state, did the trouble commence. The Zionist leaders, keeping up a pretence that they were struggling against Fascism, have been the motivators of Fascism in Palestine and have the responsibility for the heavy toll of wasted lives. Fascism? From the 'Jewish Hitler', Vladimir Jabotinsky, with his 'Storm Troop' Revisionists to the Rothschild and Imperialist Zionists in London (who take good care to keep out of the 'Holy' country), from the 'Nuremberg' laws of the synagogue to the basic ideology of Zionism (nationalism based on *race* and not on *country*) the whole of the Jewish nationalist movement has been as fascist as any other nationalist movement which has left its early liberal phase. The labour leaders like Ben Gurion accuse the Arabs of being in the pay of Hitler and Mussolini and under that pretence act the Hitlers and Mussolinis. Meanwhile they dupe the masses of Jewish workers in the pogromist countries that there is only one future — Palestine — and furnish the excuses for the anti-Semitic governments.

Undoubtedly the Arab revolution must have the support of the workers abroad. Let us not be duped as 'revolutionary socialists' have been duped, however. There is no hope for the future in a Palestine under the Grand Mufti and Company. There is no reason to suppose that a bourgeois nationalist government will do more for the working-class than did the imperialist government. The lesson of Ireland alone affords proof. The struggle must be against imperialism first, against Zionism secondly, and lastly against the bourgeois nationalist government when created.

There is no evidence that the present nationalist movement is capable of such a task. The task is to forget the past and to build up a revolutionary labour movement in Palestine, without consideration of nationality. The only hope there for workers' unity is a movement that will not include within its ranks the religious leaders of Judaism or Mohammedism, and exclusive of Jewish or Arab or British exploiters. From which side it will come remains to be seen, there is little hope for a revolution in Palestine becoming a social revolution. It may be necessary at the moment to struggle alongside the petty bourgeoisie against Imperialism, but it must be borne in mind that they can neither play a revolutionary role, and that neither the Nehrus in India nor the Muftis in Palestine can be considered as friends, but only as pawns, of the revolutionary working-class.

The programme of the new Palestinian labour movement must be for the overthrow of the Mandate; for autonomy; for a struggle against the autonomous government when created, for workers' control and freedom. The anarchist tactic for the situation in Palestine is the only road that will lead away from the present debacle; the co-operation of the Arab revolutionaries throughout the Near East, in co-operation with the anti-Zionist Jewish minority and all workers, of whatever race, will alone push forward the opportunity for a complete revolution.

25th March 1939)   ALBERT MELTZER

Victims of British Rule

ANSWERS TO QUESTIONS PUT BY CECIL WILSON, MP
Colonial Office   Rec. 6th March 1939

SCHEDULE

1. *The number of houses destroyed by order of the Government:*
   (a) Since May 1936 1024
   (b) In the year 1938 681
2. *The amount imposed in fines and the number of towns and villages involved in collective fines in connection with political disturbances:*
   (a) Since May 1936 .... LP 36,692
   (b) In the year 1938 .... LP 13,721
   (LP = Palestine Pounds)
   Two hundred and thirty four towns and villages were involved.
3. *Casualties since May 1936 to end of 1938:*

	Killed	Wounded
Arabs	752	1459
Jews	367	783
Europeans	25	25
Military	98	226

4. *Casualties for the year 1938:*

	Killed	Wounded
Arabs	503	598
Jews	255	390
Europeans	14	16
Military	63	200

	Arabs	Jews
Number of death sentences imposed since May 1936 to end of 1938	75	2
Number of death sentences imposed during 1938	63	2
Life sentences imposed since May 1936 to end of 1938	50	3
Life sentences imposed during 1938	35	3
Number in custody on 31st December 1938:		
Convicted	1185	88
Unconvicted	490	10
Detenus under the Emergency Regulations	1814	41

The Pawns in Palestine

After long deliberation the chess-players of Whitehall have made their move at last. The game that opened over twenty years ago in a brilliant and unorthodox manner, with a succession of moves by the White Knight (T. E. Lawrence) had threatened to become a stalemate. The oblique movement of the Bishop, so often a determining factor in this type of game, has proved of little value, owing to the fact that one half of the Church is immobilised and the other half moving on the wrong diagonals, the pawns being all Arabic or Jewish. The White King has now castled across the Atlantic, which may to some extent counteract possible losses resulting from the dangerous gambit contemplated next. The White Pawns (Jewish) are, if I am not mistaken about to have their ranks thinned a little to clear the ground for the White Rooks and entice the opposing pawns into a pair of breeches . . .

The 'new' policy as lined out in the White Paper of May 17th is neither pro-Arab nor pro-Jew. It is, as everybody should have expected, pro-British. Not pro-you-and-me, of course, but pro-those-people-you-read-about on the financial pages of *The Times* (though their names aren't often mentioned there) whom the directors of Rookem, Cheatem & Bashem congratulate on the large dividends paid this year plus a share bonus. That is simple enough. What will prove much more puzzling to many will be the various shrieks, yells, howls and expostulations heard from many and divers quarters. These must be explained.

It will be remembered that when the National Government introduced the India Act a few years ago and graciously accorded to India a free marionette show called the New Constitution, there was opposition from many persons who certainly had very little in common. There were, to begin with, a few who actually opposed the new constitution because it was a shameful farce intended to conceal the bloody and brutal realities of the thing we call fascism when it remains at home or the Benefits of Civilisation when we export it. Next there was the natural objection of the Labour Party because, when Ramsey MacDonald strolled into the enemy lines, he took with him all the Blue Prints for a Perfect World, this Indian Constitution being one of them. So although they obviously couldn't vote against their own Utopia they said some catty pieces about Mr MacDonald and his new friends and insinuated that the

Blue Prints were much more thumb-marked than when they had them.

But the really effective opposition came from a group of fine old crusted Tories with barnacles growing on their bottoms from ruling the seas for so many centuries without a pause. Herr Churchill was loudest among these. Lady ('Save Spain, Save Democracy') Atholl was another. In fact a considerable group of persons well known today for their love of liberty and horror of fascism opposed the Indian Constitution not because it was a racket but because they were horrified that even the appearance of democracy in India might prove the thin end of the wedge.

Turn back to Palestine. Positions have slightly changed: essentials remain. Palestine, 'The Gateway of the East', must be held — but how? By creating 'a little loyal Jewish Ulster' was the old policy. The Zionists naturally stick to that. Labour, in our changing world the champion of the Old Imperialism (especially since Mr Umbrella* found his Canossa at Munich) thinks the same way. But the 'Men on the Spot' think differently. They know the whole Arab world is up against them, determined to drive them into the sea. Adolf and Benito have their agents at work and — Oh, Boy — what a chance they've got. "The Democracy of Great Britain is your enemy — we are the enemies of the Democracy. The British socialists support imperialism and oppose your independence — we are the enemies of socialism. The Jews are the agents of this imperialism, the loyal friends of the foreign oppressors — we are the enemies of the Jews."

So the Man on the Spot feels cold feet. What if war comes? Can they hold out with the aid of their Zionist allies against a vast Arab uprising, backed by the fascist powers? Probably not. Worse news comes from India. The Muslim League are threatening. This is a serious matter, and you had better know why.

India has been held by the same strategy as Palestine. Favour a few and make them your tools. In Ireland we had Ulster, in Palestine the Jews: in India we try to keep in with the Moslems. Not very successfully, for the Moslem masses are mostly nationalist and not easily deflected from their hatred of the Raj to join in some petty feud with the Hindus. But the Moslem land-owners and upper strata have been given privileges and

[* This is a reference to the British Prime Minister at the time of Munich, Neville Chamberlain — Editor]

carefully nursed. The Muslim League is their organisation, and
very loyal on the whole to the hand that feeds it. For the Muslim
League to turn against us is rather like a mutiny in the Marines.

Here's a jam, then. The same policy that holds Palestine holds
India; but the Moslems, who are in Palestine the majority, are in
India the favoured minority. That the Moslem world is united and
that Moslems in one part of the world can feel intensely and act
fanatically when they believe Moslem interests elsewhere to be
threatened has been demonstrated dramatically — after the last
war, in the Khilafit Movement, which shook the whole of India.
To keep the goodwill of a Jewish Ulster in Palestine means losing
the last remains of our Islamic Ulster in India. And what is the use
of holding the Gateway to the East if the East itself is lost in the
process?

Hence it comes about that the principal support for a change of
policy in Palestine comes from ex-administrators of India. Let us
consider the horse first, they say, and make our plans for the stable
door in the light of these considerations. We must grant the Arabs
enough to quieten the Moslem Old Guard in India (nothing, they
know, will silence the Moslem masses but food and freedom, but
that is too much to ask . . .). Let us give the Arab potentates and
the feudal lords enough to make them our allies against this fellow
Mussolini. As to the Jews, since we may still have to fall back on
them, let immigration continue for a time: after all, within a few
years everything may have changed, and who knows but we may
find it better then to fall back on our old policy, break our
promises to the Arabs (not for the first time!) and — if we have
meanwhile defeated Germany and Italy — continue the
colonisation of Palestine without fear of the consequences?

That is what the White Paper means. Promises to the Arabs, as
vague as those we gave them in the War. For the Jews, a
temporary continuation of the colonisation policy with a threat
that if things go badly we may at the end of it throw them
overboard — hence the fury of the Zionist organisations. And for
the Powers-that-Be a temporary respite, a waiting period during
which they hope to keep both parties in Palestine guessing and on
their best behaviour, angling for the rich haul that a British
Providence may yet bestow upon good Arabs or good Jews.

Will they be good little Arabs and Jews and hang up their
stockings for Father Christmas? Will they open their mouths and
shut their eyes to see what Dame Britannia will give them?

Events to date indicate that our benevolent government has

bungled it again. The Arabs, who still want independence and self-government, seem strangely unimpressed by twelve pages of sweet nothings as a substitute. The Zionists, who are still bitterly opposed to democratic institutions which would destroy their privileged status as a minority have still no assurance that the British dictatorship will continue until the Jews have a majority — indeed, if Britain happens to keep the one specific pledge in the White Paper their minority status will be made permanent as a permanent excuse, if necessary, for the continuance of the 'Mandate'. I remember a landlord once telling me that it was "a hard life living on property". I reckon there are some at Whitehall who feel the same way about Empire. There is nothing more shocking to a real sahib than the ingratitude of the downtrodden.
3rd June 1939   REGINALD REYNOLDS

The 'Advantages' of British Imperialism

Hitler imposes a 'collective fine' on the Jews. He learnt it from the British, who have used this method for years in India and are now using it in Palestine. When an Arab village is 'collectively fined' the military and police impound all the livestock. Those who can afford to, buy back their beasts from the Government. Those who have no money lose them — that is to say, they lose their only source of livelihood, though they may be completely innocent of the 'crime' for which they are being punished. Nobody knows or cares. But the children deprived of their food, are left to starve and the parents become beggars or bandits.

The case of Palestine is an up-to-date instance of imperialism and its logical consequences. We have seen that it is as bad as fascism, if not worse. Indeed, if there is any important difference between the two systems it is that the subject peoples seem to hate imperialism a great deal more than the people of the fascist countries hate fascism! Disarmed and helpless as they are in most of the colonies, they are continually agitating and striving to organise themselves against their foreign masters.

[From *The Colonies: What Next?* by Reginald Reynolds, 1939]

2

Conspiracy on Palestine

In the year 1936 a singular case was heard in The Palestine High Court. An Arab, George Mikhail el-Qasir, sued the Attorney General of Palestine and the District Commissioner of Jaffa to prevent the demolition of his house in the Old City of Jaffa.

An official communiqué had been issued by the Government announcing the projected demolition of "certain existing buildings", ostensibly for the purpose of "opening up and improving the Old City". This sudden interest in town-planning, occurring, as it did, during the Arab General Strike, and directed against the stronghold of Arab resistance, could not fail to be regarded in quite a different light by Arabs, who were cynical enough to see in it nothing but a punitive, or — at the very least — a military, measure, directed against themselves. Unsigned handbills from the Government Press confirmed this view by hints regarding the resistance and threats of military force in the carrying out of the plan.

In the course of legal proceedings it became apparent from the evidence submitted on behalf of the Government officials that the proposed demolitions were, in fact, to be carried out by the military on instructions from the High Commissioner of Palestine. So far from being anything to do with town-planning, the destruction of these Arab houses had been ordered under an article of the Palestine (Defence) Order in Council of 1931, which said nothing about opening up or improving cities but allowed the High Commissioner to "cause any buildings to be pulled down and removed" (not blown up!) "if he thinks it necessary for the purpose of the defence of Palestine". The Article referred to

45

Regulations prescribing compensation, though, as the Chief Justice agreed, no such Regulations had in fact ever been made. In spite of this stipulation a notice served on the petitioner, requiring him to vacate his house, informed him that "No claim for compensation in respect of furniture or effects left in your house after that hour" (7 pm on 28th June) "will be considered".

This case was heard before the Chief Justice, Sir Michael McDonnell and the Senior Puisne Judge, Mr. Justice Manning. Though concurring completely in their findings, the two judges prepared separate judgements on the case owing, as the Chief Justice remarked, to its "seriousness and importance". Whilst giving the judgement against the Petitioner (for the Government had, apparently, a legal "right" to blow up every house in Palestine if it thought fit) the judges "marked their disapproval by doing so without costs" and some memorable observations were made on the administration and its methods. The Chief Justice said:

"The Petitioner, however, has done a public service in exposing what I am bound to call the singularly disingenuous lack of moral courage displayed by the Administration in the whole matter . . .

It would have been more creditable if the Government, instead of endeavouring to throw dust in people's eyes by professing to be inspired by aesthetic or other quasi-philanthropic motives, such as those concerned with town planning or public health . . . had said frankly and truthfully that it was primarily for defensive purposes."

Mr. Justice Manning was even more explicit. Mr. Kantovorich, the Junior Government advocate, had appeared for the defendants and excused the deception, or attempted deception, of the people of Jaffa by explaining that they would have been "misled" if the truth had been told them. The comments of Mr. Justice Manning were caustic in the extreme: "We would have misled them by telling them the truth, so we thought it better to tell them a falsehood" — such was his paraphrase of the case for the defence.

The proposed demolition was, in fact, only legal on the assumption that its ostensible excuse was a pack of lies: and Mr. Justice Manning summed up his reason for giving his judgement against the Petitioner in these words:

"I feel bound to accept the statement of the Government that the proposed demolition was always intended to be carried out under the provisions of the Order-in-Council and that this was concealed from the inhabitants of Jaffa because, not being lawyers, they might not have understood it. This is what Mr. Kantrovitch has said. In this particular instance I can conceive that the inhabitants affected might be bewildered by being told that the destruction of their houses was necessary for the defence of Palestine, and that their houses could be blown up when there was power only to pull them down."

After illustrating from the damage anticipated to neighbouring houses the difference between power to blow up and power to pull down, Mr. Justice Manning concluded with a reference to

"a well-known work of fiction which described a Government Department known as the Circumlocution Office . . . Something similar seems to have found its way into Palestine, but its identity has been carefully concealed."

Some 250 houses were destroyed in Jaffa, and other buildings were damaged by the explosions. No provision was made for housing those who were rendered homeless, and on this subject a scathing report was issued by the Government Welfare Officer (Miss Margaret Nixon). Whatever effect the High Court Judgement had in restoring confidence in British "justice" was negatived by a policy of wholesale demolitions throughout the country and other repressive measures. Even the two courageous judges were made to feel the weight of administrative censure for their outspoken comments. The Chief Justice was offered the choice of an inferior appointment in a British colony or retirement on a pension — he chose the latter. His colleague, Mr. Justice Manning, who might have been expected to succeed him, was soon after this transferred, and the post of Chief Justice was filled by the Attorney General, a man named Trusted, who was one of the defendants in this celebrated case and (as the Government's legal advisor) had been chiefly responsible for the "evasiveness" which the judges had condemned. A final postscript might record the re-appearance of Sir Michael McDonnell, the ex-Chief Justice of Palestine, as Chairman of one of the London Appelate Tribunals for Conscientious Objectors. It is not within my present scope to discuss why a man who was found too just for Palestine is not considered too just for his present position; but one may remark in passing that it is evidence of the Government's intention to avoid filling up its jails by a judicious sorting of objectors. Which shows that even the worst government may find a use for a just judge!

The real importance of this case is that it should be necessary to recall it at all. The reader may judge for himself that such sweeping criticism of a Government by the Chief Justice, in concurrence with a colleague, made in a High Court judgement should normally make the case a *cause celebre* and insure the widest possible publicity. Quite the most interesting thing about this case is that no such publicity followed it. To the best of my knowledge, not a single British newspaper even mentioned it. The British administration in a British Mandate stood condemned by British judges, in a British Court, of deliberate falsehood and a cowardly attempt at deception; but the people of Britain — the great "democracy" on which there lay the final responsibility for the welfare of that "sacred trust of civilisation" — did not know and to this day still do not know that their officials were convicted of lying and cowardice. Still less do they know that those who found them out were punished and that the man principally responsible for the Government's policy in this matter was rewarded with high office, so that the future Chief Justice might be less difficult to deal with.

This story aptly illustrates the blanket of concealment and deception which has characterised British administration in Palestine more than any other aspect of British Imperialism. It is in itself a story of attempted deception and it ends with a conspiracy of the entire British press to prevent that story even reaching the British public. It is, in fact, an epitome of our relations with the Arabs — first deceive the Arabs, or try to; then deceive the British public by hushing up the attempted deception of the Arabs.

The story begins with our promises to the Arabs during the first world war. There has been endless argument about what those promises actually meant; and though — having studied the correspondence — I consider the Arabs case to be indisputable, the alternative proposition, which is that our promises were ambiguous, is hardly to our credit. What is even more sinister, and beyond argument, is that the text of that correspondence *was never published by the British Government in full* until the Palestine Conference in London before the present war. Then at last, forced by crisis and imminent danger in the Near East, the Government yielded to the Arab demand that the full correspondence should be published, with official translations of Arabic texts. For over twenty years successive British Governments concealed that correspondence from British 'democracy' and from the outside world, to the best of their ability.

What our government could *not* conceal, however, were the

terms laid down in President Wilson's 'Fourteen Points'. Point 12 stated that "The Turkish portions of the present Ottoman Empire should be assured a secure sovereignty, but *the other nationalities which are now under Turkish rule should be assured* an undoubted security of life and *an absolutely unmolested opportunity of autonomous development*" (my own italics). The 'Fourteen Points' were not accepted without reservations by the Allied Powers; but these reservations were explicitly stated in a note from Mr. Lansing (then American Secretary of State) to the Minister for Foreign Affairs at Berne, on 6th November 1918. Indeed, Mr. Lloyd George, in a speech on War Aims (5th January 1918) had already declared that "a territorial settlement must be secured, based on *the right of self-determination or the consent of the governed*".

The Palestine 'Mandate' may therefore be said to have come into existence in defiance of the Covenant of the League of Nations itself, according to which Palestine, as an 'A' Mandate, should have received only such outside advice and assistance as the people required and asked for from a Mandatory Power of their own selection. Instead of this, the country has been governed as a colony, used as a military, air and naval base in time of war, and forcibly subjected to immigration on an unprecedented scale. A country about the size of Wales, without the inhabitants being consulted, has been forced to absorb some 400,000 immigrants, whose most powerful political organisations have bitterly opposed even the most timid moves towards self-government that would allow the Arab majority any real control of their own country and its resources.

Sympathy with the Jews, persecuted in so many other countries, has completely blinded 'left' opinion to this iniquity and helped to wrap the blanket of deceit and falsehood even closer around the problem of Palestine. One would have thought that, in such countries as the USA, Canada, Australia, New Zealand, the states of South America and even in Britain, those who felt most strongly the hardships of the Jews would wish to share their own heritage rather than thrust the Jews upon a country which has never asked for them, creating a new problem to solve an old one, saving people from oppression to make them instruments for the oppression of others. But this is not the case. As recently as May 1941 an article by Middleton Murry* was reprinted in *The Adelphi*

[* Editor of *Peace News* at the time — Editor]

which reflects the widespread ignorance in pacifist circles regarding the implications of the Palestine Mandate and of Zionism in particular. Under the title 'Meditation on Heine' the writer discusses the Jewish problem in a sympathetic manner to which one can take no exception until he mentions Palestine. The article, it is true, was originally written and published in 1934; but neither then nor now could Mr. Murry's words show the slightest realisation of what has actually happened in the Much Promised Land. He speaks of "Jewish Palestine" in which anti-Semitism finds its "counter-assertion", which here "takes a noble, creative and regenerative form". There is no recognition that Zionism has stirred up more anti-Jewish feeling than all the propaganda of Julius Streicher — I will not say "anti-Semitism" for the Arabs themselves are Semites! Mr. Murry finds in Zionism "the permanent conquest of a Mediterranean shore for the 'European' idea" — and cannot see that this "conquest" (permanent or otherwise) can hardly be welcomed by those who are of the 'conquered' race. And lest we should imagine that this is indeed a conquest purely of ideas, and not, as it is in fact, a forcible colonisation of a foreign country, Middleton Murry even says, "I am heartily glad that this has been done beneath our aegis". *Our aegis* is surely a mild expression for imprisonments and executions, internments without trial, collective fines, the wholesale destruction of houses, martial law and the rest of the reign of terror which has been necessary to curb Arab resentment and make possible the policies of British imperialists and their Zionist allies. But when a distinguished pacifist can write in this way we have conclusive proof of the successful way in which the whole problem has been blanketed.

A final instance must conclude this very brief study of the way in which the facts about Palestine are distorted or suppressed. Years ago I used to say that it was hard to get adequate publicity for the social conditions of our own country, harder still if one linked these facts with any form of socialist criticism, and all but impossible — in most vehicles of news and opinion — if one discussed British imperialism in India or the colonies. The pre-war years offered, in this respect, a marked contrast between the readiness of the press to lap up propaganda directed against German or Italian fascism and the *decreasing* attention to the worst evils of fascism when they appeared in some part of the British Empire. But at that time I discovered a singular fact — that, hard as it was to obtain a hearing for the wrongs suffered by

Indians or Negroes, the hardest thing of all was to obtain the slightest attention to those suffered by the Palestine Arabs. *The boycott was almost complete.*

I therefore conclude with a copy of a letter which I sent to the *New Statesman* on 4th May of the present year. The *Statesman* is generally ready to publish views, even on the British Empire and the war, with which it is in disagreement. That this letter remained unpublished, whilst Zionist letters appeared and remained unanswered may be taken as a typical example of how even the more 'left' papers are involved in this conspiracy on Palestine. I give the text of the letter in full because, apart from the fact that it shows just what was suppressed, the case as I have outlined it here is still urgently relevant to the present situation. It is probably too late now to hope that the catastrophe foreseen by many of us long before the war will be averted; but it is *not* too late, nor yet too early, to work for a new attitude towards the whole problem of imperialism, of which Palestine is such an outstanding example. the betrayals of the past, the deceit and camouflage of the present, should accustom us to expect more deceit and fresh betrayals, to anticipate no more from the flimsy 'war aims' of today than we reaped from the perjured promises of yesterday. We must be ready, whatever the upshot of this war, for more fine phrases, as reassuring as those of the late President Wilson — *and refusing to be reassured in the least, we must prepare now for the real struggle which this war cannot settle and will only complicate further.* This rejected letter was intended, and is still intended, to throw a little light on at least one corner of a tortured world, the history of which has been tragedy and the future of which will be nemesis. *Unless we understand our responsibilities for the past we are never likely to face our responsibilities for the future.*

My letter to the *New Statesman* read as follows:

"In your editorial of May 3rd you refer to the Foreign Office having conciliated 'the reactionaries — The Fifth Column among the Arab magnates of Palestine and Irak'.

I do not understand this statement or the assertion that we have 'cold shouldered and neglected' the Palestine Jews. Whatever may be said for or against Zionism, it was an immigration carried out without reference to the wishes of the people of the country, and, judging by the history of Palestine under the Mandate, in direct opposition to those wishes. From the end of the last war the Arabs have been treated to a haphazard mixture of repression and promises, and the demand of Arab 'reactionaries' for democratic self-government in Palestine remains unfulfilled.

On the other hand, the Jewish immigrants, forced upon the country and remaining there under the protection of British bayonets, can hardly complain of their treatment in general. They have successfully opposed even the most timid moves towards representative government and have established a minority interest which has been maintained in defiance of majority rights by such 'democratic' measures as internment of Arabs without trial and wholesale destruction of Arab houses (to mention only two indisputable facts regarding our stewardship).

We are told that the Arab leaders are feudal reactionaries. If that be so, then the same could be said of the authors of Magna Carta and of Simon de Montfort (who persecuted the Jews!) whilst Pym and Hampden can be regarded merely as representatives of a reactionary squirearchy. History, however, is right in regarding such men as instruments in a progressive process rather than as individuals with discreditable motives. One would have thought that in the present case, the cause of self-determination was of greater importance than the conjectures as to the motives of a few leaders.

If the Arabs today are inclined to listen favourably to Hitler, who's is the fault? Have they such pleasant experiences of British 'democracy' and of British 'socialists' (pro-Zionist almost to a man) or of the Jews themselves? Hitler, as the avowed enemy of democracy, Socialism, and the Jews, must inevitably have his attractions in a country where 'democracy', 'socialism' and Zionism have been cloaks for imperialist policies. Not only in Palestine, but throughout the Arab world, there are Arabs who feel keenly on these questions. It is no doubt very foolish of them to hope for better things from Hitler, but at least it is understandable, *and the blame is on us.*

Many Arabs are turning to Hitler, just as those other 'reactionary feudalists' — the Abyssinians — turned to Britain for help against Italy, or as the Arabs themselves once sought a British alliance against Turkey. Unless unforeseen events upset my calculations, the Abyssinians are about to be 'sold a pup' by our government, and the Arabs will be cheated as badly by Hitler as they were on the previous occasion by Britain. But the fate of the Jews in Palestine is even more certain if Hitler breaks through into that part of the world; and whose fault will it be? Who but ourselves fostered and encouraged the Zionist policy, deliberately creating 'a Jewish Ulster', as it was called by Sir Ronald Storrs? Who but the Zionists themselves consistently opposed self-government and, by their policies, made friendly relations on a basis of equality impossible between Jew and Arab? I ask these questions deliberately in anticipation of events which may appal public opinion here — not to excuse or justify but to *explain* Arab resentment. Again and again the Palestine Jews have been warned that their insistence on their own minority interests as vastly more important than the rights of the Arab majority would lead to their isolation, to a bitter racial feud and to their ultimate extinction. These were not threats — men like Dr. Magnus (himself an eminent Jewish scholar) repeated such statements as sober warnings and solemn prophesies.

I write today in the consciousness that nothing has been done to avert such a tragedy and that, should my own worst fears be realised, few in England will stop to think how near our own doorstep lies the prime responsibility. So far from having erred by 'conciliating' the Arabs, I hold that the double crime of British imperialism in Palestine has been the repression of the Arabs and fostering among the Jews unrealisable hopes which have lured them steadily to their own destruction."

This article will be denounced by many as 'anti-Semitic'. As I have already pointed out, an Arab is also a Semite. My position, in fact, is (oddly enough) that I am opposed to the oppression of anybody by anybody else. And my attitude to Jews, Arabs and every other nation is determined by what those particular Arabs, Jews, Germans or Englishmen happen to be doing. Sympathy with Indians and indignation on account of their sufferings does not make me a lover of Indian princes — quite the reverse. And that man is a sentimental nuisance who lets his sympathy with the persecuted Jews colour his attitude to the oppressive and suicidal policy of Zionism and the gigantic fraud which has so long successfully concealed the operations of British imperialism in Palestine.

August 1941   REGINALD REYNOLDS

Palestine and the Jews

I

To civilised people today the position of the Jews is intolerable. In increasing numbers of countries the centuries' plague of the ghetto and the pogrom is reviving. Against the mediaeval curse of anti-semitism, on the one hand, and the inevitable Jewish reaction to its own nationalism on the other, there must be some method of struggle.

What is the method advocated by liberals and the left today? In the main it is agreed: the re-establishment of

religious and racial tolerance in all countries, on the one hand; and the establishment of the Zionist aim — a Jewish National Home — in Palestine, on the other.

It is perhaps necessary to give first the background of Zionism, and the reasons why Zionism came into conflict with the Arabs in Palestine.

The first modern exponent of Zionism was Theodore Herzl. Moved by growing anti-semitic feeling in France and in his native Austria, and later by the feeling of sympathy with the persecuted Russian Jews felt by all sections, Herzl evolved his plan of a Jewish State. His idea was that the Jews could form a small nation somewhere in the world, and so end the national distinctions pervading amongst the Jews themselves.

It is sometimes said by Zionists today that Palestine was the end-all and be-all of Jewish hope and aspirations for centuries. This is not so. True, the Jewish religion has centred around the idea of 'the Promised Land' which the Jews would re-enter but it was thought that only Messianic times would see the 'Chosen people' arrive in Jerusalem. In short, the rabbinical idea of the 'New Jerusalem' was pretty much the same as the Christian. (The prayer concluding 'Next year — in Jerusalem!', for instance, has always been and still is used by Jews *in* Jerusalem, too.) Only the portents announced in the Talmud could herald the return of the Jews to the 'Promised Land,' and in fact the Jewish religion thought of Palestine as a spiritual, not a material, concept.

Prior to Herzl, hardly anyone ever dreamt of an actual return of the Jews to Palestine, and when Herzl's plan was published, its fiercest opponents were the rabbis, it being contrary to all their teaching. They cast doubts on Herzl's orthodoxy, helped by the fact that, like so many Austrian Jews, his father was a convert to Christianity and Herzl had been brought up as a Christian, returning to Judaism later in life. (It was asked contemptuously if Herzl considered himself King David!)

In addition to incurring the opposition of religious Judaism, Zionism was frowned on or ignored by the rich and powerful Jews, who naturally had no wish to see the *status quo* upset.

Herzl's scheme might have appealed to the homeless, hungry and persecuted Jews of Russia. But a vague promised land had nothing on a definite Promised Land — America! Like the rest of Europe's downtrodden they looked to the symbol of liberty that to Europe's millions was represented by the United States. The acute labour shortage following the Civil War gave rise to a demand for labour — for immigrants — and the immigrants came in their thousands; Jews from the pogrom countries with the thousands of Italians, Irish, Latvians, Armenians, Poles, Czechs and the rest.

It rather seemed at first as if Herzl was to enjoy only the support of a handful of Jewish intellectuals and a number of influential anti-Semites (many of whom strongly advocated the acceding by the French Government of a plot of land in Africa for the settlement of the Jews — willy-nilly). At first the Zionists listened to the schemes of settlement in Africa, but under the influence of Herzl turned down all such promises. The choice was finally made — Palestine only. In this Herzl made a tactical move. He gave his movement a solid basis, by gaining religious Jewish support. While for long the orthodox opposition on the grounds that re-settlement in Palestine prior to the Messiah's belated arrival was contrary to teachings, the rabbis were shrewd enough to realise that their shibboleths were crumbling, not against persecution but against tolerance. America, the 'melting pot' of all nations, was assimilating its Jewish citizens too. The same process was at work in South Africa, in Britain, in France, in Germany. Jews were losing their identity as Jews. Most of them were unable to believe in the God of their fathers (any more than their Gentile neighbours) they were forgetting the old codes and taboos. A 'religious revival' was the Gentile reaction to 19th century agnosticism. This in turn passed to Fascism. With the Jews it was similar. The rabbis looked to a mystical nationalism, such as Herzl was advocating.

It cannot be said that the majority of Jews who pioneered Zionism in Palestine were orthodox Jews. Other than the Polish and Russian Jews, there were few orthodox Jews left. Palestine since has not been a home for orthodoxy. A modern Palestine Jew would not at all bother about a pork dinner in the shadow of the Wailing Wall. But orthodoxy has gathered more strength; and while it has not produced its goal — a Jewish religion and race separated from all others — it has helped to produce a separatist feeling amongst nationalist Jews that may (with or without the religious stimulus) have far-reaching effects. In all this the whole outlook of Zionism was and is essentially reactionary and of a fascist nature. Prior to his aping Hitler's anti-semitism, the Revisionists (right wing Zionist extremists) did indeed look on Mussolini as an inspired statesman.

On the other hand, it is unquestionable that side by side with the pipe-dreams of a Messianic Jewish community in the Near East, and the nationalist aspirations of others, there existed a number of Jews who, with no sympathy with their abandoned religion, hoped Zionism might be a symbol of regeneration. It may not be altogether possible for Gentile readers to appreciate how bitterly they detested the racketeering elements who figured so prominently in the early days of South Africa. The entirely unscrupulous Rand financiers were too often Jews. A product of the inferiority complex engendered by separatism, and of the city, the gambling mob that disgraced itself was unquestionably regarded by large numbers of decent Jews as 'the type of Jew who causes anti-semitism.' To get away from this city bred type they did hope for a national regeneration on the land. 'To get back to the land' — 'regeneration on the soil' — It is the usual mystical nonsense that has a great appeal to people who themselves have not experienced the narrowness of life in an agricultural community, but so far as it was a reaction it was progressive.

The above gives a clear picture of the whole tenor of Jewry prior to the 1914 war.[1]

The Balfour Declaration gave the Jews the right to a National Home in Palestine. While promising the Arabs and other subject peoples of the decaying Ottoman Empire full liberty in the post war world (added to the specious promises made by Lawrence and others) the idea of a Jewish State in Palestine was given life (which to the majority of people, including most Jews, was as fanciful a project as the establishment of an Eireann state in Ireland, with the old Gaelic language — or, since this too happened after the war — as if Sweden suddenly went Viking).

Why was the declaration made? It must have been realised that the Arabs, when free of Turkish rule, would not voluntarily submit to any other foreign domination. But, since it was decided that this strategically important country must be in the jurisdiction of the British Empire (to safeguard the route to India and the Orient), some plan had to be evolved of colonising the country in part. Evidently the British Government was influenced by the Zionist minority in agreeing to the idea of a Jewish Home in Palestine. The only alternative (in fact) was to settle emigrants generally, as in South Africa and Australia. But British emigrants were few (as

---

1. The interested reader will find profitable study in many of the novels of Israel Zangwill ('The King of Schnorrers', 'Children of the Ghetto', etc.) whose pen has made a truly Dickensian survey.

colonial experience had shown): and it may well be that European emigrants were simply not trusted. Already in Canada and Australia the door was barred to the 'teeming millions' of European immigration.[2] In Palestine, too: none but the 'reliable'.

The British Government was assured of Jewish reliability. While the Arabs could not be trusted from an Imperial standpoint (they would, like the Egyptians, raise awkward questions about autonomy) the war had proved that the Jewish community would respond to a patriotic demand. The majority of British Jews were viewed with suspicion at the commencement of the war of 1914. The fact that a majority of them were foreign born, and the anti-immigration agitation of the 1890s had been mostly anti-semitic rather than anti-foreign, was an incentive to the suspicion against them. Looting of shops bearing German names soon spread to looting of shops bearing Jewish — even Russian (then Allied) names! The Jews had, however, not been provoked; had supported the war like the other communities.

Prominent in recruiting campaigns was the Chief Rabbi (Austrian born, and therefore an 'enemy alien'. The German Chief Rabbi was also an 'enemy alien' being Russian born!). Jews were volunteering and being drafted into the army. But even more there had to be considered the tradition of the upper class Jews, which naturally had more influence on the Government. The Disraeli tradition persisted in Lord Reading, there were the Rothschild and Sassoon dynasties, men such as Lord Burnham (founder of *The Daily Telegraph*) the circle of Edward VII, the Montefiore family and others — the existence of whom assured the British Government of two things:

(1) that the leaders of British Jewry could be trusted to influence the remainder into supporting any Imperial designs in Palestine, and in regulating the European Jewish immigrants into that country along the same road. (Foremost among the 'safe men' chosen for the regulation of Palestine was, of course, Lord Reading; the prominent bourgeois statesman whose administration in Palestine, as in India, combined 'reconciliation' with implicit obedience to Imperialist dictates).

---

2. The U.S.A., when padlocking the doors to the European immigration that evolved it, gave the reason in its notorious declaration that all persons entering the U.S.A. (even on a visit) are compelled to make — one effectively ruling out anarchists, radicals, — even democrats!

(2) that since the position of Jews in most countries was, following the changes made by the war, favourable, (and the Versailles Treaty was to last a thousand years!) only a minority of Jews from the ever-decreasing pogrom countries, plus a few Zionist idealists, plus some British Jews seeking administrative positions, would enter Palestine.

Hence immigration was intended to be controlled, regulated and shepherded into a steady colonising trickle that would act as a safeguard against anti-imperialist designs of the Arabs; would colonise the country; would build a European community able to commercialise the assets of the country and at the same time guard against foreign aggression towards the oil-fields of the Middle East, and the route to India.

At first Arab objection as such to the 'Jewish National Home' did not arise. There was some Moslem rioting in Jerusalem in connection with the alleged 'Holy Places' — but in Jerusalem, the 'City of Peace' there has always been rioting over that! Trouble began first when the colonial enterprise became profitable, owing to the cupidity of both Jewish capitalists and Arab landowners.

Jewish capitalists from America were interested in the commercial proposition. They were building new industries and new towns. Tel-Aviv, for instance, rose from nothing to a new Chicago; farms appeared on what was once desert; Jerusalem, from being a sleepy Turkish provincial town where the different Christian priests quarrelled over their rights, became a hive of twentieth century industry. The Dead Sea became a live centre for tourists. In short, Palestine was being developed in the same way as South Africa had been, only in a much more rapid process. Unfortunately, contrary to the opinions of idealists who had hoped to pioneer an agricultural socialism, the same faults and methods of colonisation appeared in Palestine as in South Africa. (It is sometimes argued, of course, that capitalists coming into a country and colonising it develop the land 'and make work for the natives', an even more ironical statement than the old anti-socialist story that 'the capitalist puts up the capital without which the worker could not work; hence the worker lives on the capitalist, not vice versa!')

As for the Arab landowners, they were no less culpable than the Jewish capitalists. They sold their land at high prices to the investors, stretching the price to the highest conceivable limit because of the need for land, knowing full well what the sale of land would mean to their own peasants. Having forced the

peasants off the land which they had sold at high prices to the
Jewish investors, they told the peasants that the Jews had stolen
the land, and carried on a political agitation to win back the land
— in order to sell it again.

By virtue of their ties with Mohammedanism, the Arab
landowners were able to influence the British Government. They
were politically identical with the 'Muslim League' minority in
India, representing as it does the landowning and financial clique,
and not the Arab peasants.

However, in saying that the Arab landowners took advantage of
the Jewish influx to sell their land at high prices, and force down
the standard of life of the peasant, this does not mean that it was
not the case that the Arab peasant was forced off his land. The
Jewish capitalist, and (playing a double game) the Arab
landowner, were responsible. But because nationalist feeling is
what it is, the Arab peasant thought of only the Jewish capitalist —
and hence all Jews — as responsible. This explains the whole
feeling of the Arab peasant. Led by a corrupt gang under the
Grand Mufti, he could only see the whole thing as a national feud
— Arab versus Jew.

In the same way, the average Jewish immigrant was not able to
appreciate any reason for the disturbances that arose with intensity
each year, culminating in the struggles of the late 'thirties. He
came from Roumania, or Poland, or Hungary, where it was not
unexpected for a sudden pogrom against the Jews. Escaping from
his country, he arrived in Palestine, hoping to form a nation of his
own. On arriving in Palestine, he found the Arabs incensed at the
arrival of Jewish immigrants, hostile to the outlying settlements,
unfriendly, and finally openly taking to arms. What could he
think, except that the pogrom spirit had followed him across
Europe to the 'Promised Land'? What alternative could he see
except the continuance of the national feud?

In short the Jewish immigrant was brought over on a short term
policy of the Jewish capitalist: and the capitalist was aided by the
Arab landowners to force out the Arab peasant.

A.M.

II

The policy pursued in Palestine, therefore, could only lead to
disaster. The Arab peasants were forced off the land, and saw
relief only in the national feud. There was a section that saw relief
in assistance from the Axis powers, "since they too were against
the Jews" (Quite obviously this was nonsense; European
anti-semitism would speed up Jewish immigration into Palestine
rather than the reverse. The Axis was interested in fostering its
agents amongst this section because of the very tactical nature of
Palestine in the Mediterranean, rather than from any motives of
ideology). There were also the wealthy Arabs who looked forward
to a scheme of division, in which their own future would be
assured, by the scarcity of land and hence its high market value.
(This scheme, roughly resembling the "Pakistan" of some of Mr.
Jinnah's followers in India, but in a much smaller country, would
have allowed so many cantons on the Swiss model to Jews and so
many to Arabs). The whole civil war that blazed up in Palestine
was in the last analysis vain; because the nationalist leaders would
not in any case have looked for sole independence, but merely an
end of the system of colonisation being pursued.

On the Jewish side, the persecutions breaking out again in
Europe had brought a large-scale immigration to Palestine. For a
long time Hitler permitted the Zionist organisation to exist, and it
enjoyed the unenviable position of being the only non-Nazi
political organisation in Germany tolerated by the State. The
leaders of Jewish communities, particularly in America, accentu-
ated the efforts to get Jewish families out of Germany, especially
into Palestine. The British Government, which had never foreseen
such a move, was reluctant to permit this, particularly since it did
not wish to disturb the situation in Palestine any more. The whole
effect of the Palestine experiment so far as the victims of Hitlerism
were concerned was to raise a false chimera of hope before them,
of allaying anti-Nazi feeling which would have broken out in
Germany itself on this issue had not the Jewish homelessness been
explained away by "but the Jews have somewhere to go — it's the
British government that prevents it," and most of all it encouraged
the Governments that wished to have an excuse not to admit
immigrants themselves; but to express their desire for the refugees
to enter somewhere — in particular, the American government.

Can the Zionist Experiment be Pursued Further?

It does not seem as if abandonment of Zionism is anyone's war aims. The British Government no doubt intends to continue as before, allowing a trickle of immigration, not to disturb its present basis. Hitler too wants a Ghetto State — a Jewish 'Pale of Settlement', but apparently in the worst areas of Poland. Palestine itself is no doubt regarded by the Nazis as a vital link which they would colonise themselves. In short, a Nazi victory in the war would mean the re-colonisation of Palestine, and the position in a few years' time would be similar to today. An oppressed Arab population would be still struggling for independence.

A British victory no doubt means the status quo in Palestine. But we havé the usual claims on the Government, and policy may be influenced in one or the other direction. Ever since the war began the Revisionists, and later most Zionists, have been clamouring for a 'Jewish Army' in Palestine, with its own flag, its own divisions, its own commanders, on a level with other Allied nations. In vain has the Government explained that there is no Jewish State, that Jews are citizens of other States, consequently Jews can only be soldiers of the armies of the Allied Governments and not of their own non-existent Government. There is no pressing demand by Jews in the ranks to have their own Army, why therefore create one? Yet the demand persists, especially from American Jews (Dr Abba Silver is at the moment in England on this very mission). The answer is obvious. They want a Jewish army based on Palestine as the thin edge of the wedge for a Jewish State based on Palestine.

Why should this demand be so popular amongst American Jews? They have no disabilities in America; there is no urgent need for an exodus of Jewish refugees from New York; the problems of European anti-semitism do not affect them. It must be admitted that American Jews thinking of the creation of a State in Palestine have no intention of taking its citizenship themselves. They want to see the State, but with citizens strictly limited to those from Europe. They cannot see that actually they themselves are preparing the ground for American anti-semitic laws.

For essentially the whole prospect of Zionism for the Jews is as unsatisfactory as it is for the Arabs. The exclusion of the latter from their homes is equally balanced by the exclusion of the former. The gainer in each case is the coloniser and the landlord; and the loser both the immigrant worker and the native peasant.

The kind of Zionism envisaged before the war meant essentially co-operation with Hitler and other anti-semitic rulers. The kind of Zionism envisaged for after the war means that it is considered that anti-semitism will still prevail in the countries from which the settlers are emigrating.

The solution of Jewish miseries in the world to-day does not therefore lie in Zionism (nationalism); it lies in the fight against anti-semitism, and hence the *fight against nationalism*.

In the last analysis, the solution to the whole problem of Jewish homelessness and persecution, lies in the solution to the problem of the workers everywhere: i.e., the building of a world freed from nationalism and States.

But it may be asked, can this particular problem wait? No problem can wait. A desirable conclusion may have to wait, but the means of action must be taken now.

In Palestine

It is clearly difficult and nearly impossible for the anti-Zionist Jew in Palestine itself to take action. He not only incurs the hostility of the majority of other Jews, but cannot allay the suspicion of the majority of Arabs. But an anti-Zionist minority, and a class-conscious Arab minority too, can grow, and from the nucleus of a minority of revolutionary Jews and Arabs can grow a movement with the main principles:

(a) the abandonment of the Zionist State experiment on the one hand, and of an Arabic kingdom on the other;

(b) anti-Imperialism, opposition to external capitalism and internal landlordism;

(c) disregard for the religious scruples causing a barrier amongst the people;

(d) the struggle for an independent workers' country, to take its place amongst other independent workers' countries of the new world, on the same principles of revolutionary libertarian socialism (and with absolute disregard for race).

I do not say such a minority with such a programme is an immediate likelihood, but it is towards the creation of such a minority that the policy of revolutionary workers elsewhere must be. It would not matter whether such a movement were inaugurated solely by Jews or solely by Arabs; the point is that such a movement can arise to take in all of whatever nationality. It is by aiming at such a movement, and not by supporting any propositions which may come from interested parties during this war, that the revolutionary workers may know they are not being misled by false nationalist divisions once again.

On the question of Arab independence: it may be that Arab revolutionaries would feel themselves bound to a movement of Arab independence, similar to Indian and Moroccan revolutionaries. We agree, it may sometimes be necessary to go part of the way with colonial bourgeois nationalists; but our aim in all cases is to expose the leaders of the colonial peoples, and point the way to their own emancipation. The support of any independence movement should not therefore prejudice the main object, that of a movement of all the toilers.

In the Rest of the World

This may well point to a course of action for the Jews of Palestine, but it will be argued that the Jews in the pogrom countries will be left without hope, except with the hope of far-off revolution. In the first place, this is an improvement, for even the *hope* of a revolution and a free system of society in the future is more practicable than the hope of a peaceful national state, when one views the position of all other small states, in far less strategic positions.

Moreover the course of revolution can be pursued, but as the 'Struma' tragedy shows, the Governments of the world have no intention of letting immigration be pursued. It may be that Herschel Grynspan, before the war, had a clearer notion than many of the worthies who washed their hands of him, as to how the pogrom governments should be fought. It was better to have struck at Vom Rath than to have committed suicide, at least; and while perhaps it did not accomplish much — had not Grynspan been denounced so readily by those who wished to show they had nothing to do with it — the example might have been contagious.

We do not have to go into details to show that fascism can be fought from within. It goes equally to show that anti-semitism is a product of capitalist and nationalist society, and that it can be equally fought with the system by the revolutionary workers; that in fact, a government cannot impose it without the aid of the masses (as witness Holland, Denmark and Norway, countries where the virus of anti-semitism had never infected the masses, and where the Nazis have been unable to carry through the Nuremberg laws).

Countering nationalism with nationalism does not solve a

national problem. The revolutionary class struggle does. Anti-semitism will finally be smashed by the revolutionary class struggle, if pursued logically. And the logical course of the class struggle is not to confuse anti-semitism with anti-Zionism. The former is reactionary, but the latter is one of the means of fighting the former.

mid-March/April 1942   ALBERT MELTZER

Refugee Ship Sunk

Government Responsibility

Last month a small cargo boat carrying 750 Jewish refugees from central Europe blew up and sank in the Black Sea off the coast of Turkey. Five survivors reached the shore, but of these three died of exposure; only two out of the original 750 escaped the tragedy. There is no information as to their subsequent fate.

Although most sections of the press mentioned the sinking of the 'Struma', few went into any details or attempted to assess the responsibility. Here are the outlines of the story.

The 'Struma' carried 769 Jewish refugees — men, women and children — from Rumania and Bulgaria, and sailed under the Panamanian flag. The refugees hoped to be admitted into Palestine. They arrived at Istambul on 15th December 1941, and lay there for two months under conditions of food and sanitation described as desperate.

The immigration schedule allows 3,000 Jews to enter Palestine during the current six months, and the Jewish Agency made every effort to persuade the Palestine Administration to admit them. Meanwhile the Joint American Distribution Committee offered not only to pay all expenses incurred, but to give a subsidy of £6,000 for training those capable of entering industry. The Palestine authorities, however, refused to consider the claims of even those who had relatives already in the country and now serving with the British forces in the Near East. The matter was then taken up with the Colonial Office in London. Two arguments were advanced by the British authorities for refusing permission to those 769 refugees to enter Palestine. First, that they were enemy aliens, having been under the Nazis, and therefore there might be enemy agents among them. The Jewish Agency repeatedly pointed out that they could be placed in internment camps until their bona fides had been investigated. Needless to say this argument had no effect since the whole excuse was manifestly a cover for simple refusal on the part of the British to accept these refugees. The fact that they had already suffered under Antonescu's anti-semitic terror simply had no effect at all on the officials concerned. The second 'reason' put forward for not admitting them was that "there was a shortage of supplies to Palestine." Comment is scarcely required, but the Jewish Agency nevertheless pointed out that under the schedule 3,000 Jews were to be admitted during the current six months. In WAR COMMENTARY we recently quoted an extract showing the glut of products normally exported from Palestine now rotting on the trees there. This glut is termed by the British as a "shortage of supplies."

At the last minute the authorities gave permission for the children under 16 to be admitted. This decision, however, was not made known until after the Turkish government had ordered the ship to leave Turkish territorial waters. These children therefore went down with the rest.

The British authorities (and the Turkish government) were of course fully aware that in the event of permission to enter Palestine being refused, the ship with its cargo of Jewish refugees would have to return to Rumania, to the anti-semitic regime from which they had attempted to escape. The refusal of permission amounted therefore to co-operation with the Rumanian authorities (with whom, be it noted, the British government is at war) in the apprehension of these Jews who had managed to escape abroad. Not only did the British authorities show themselves to be entirely indifferent to the tragic plight of these wretched fugitives from fascist terror, but they were even cynical enough to display no show of zeal to implement all their promises of putting an end to the persecution of minorities under fascism. They have shown what their much publicised indignation (in the Government's White Paper on *The Treatment of German Nationals* and the persecutions in Poland, for instance) really amounts to, when it comes to offering comparative safety to a mere 750 odd refugees.

It has been suggested that the blowing up of the 'Struma' was not due to a mine, as was first reported, but was the work of the refugees themselves; they preferred to blow themselves up to returning to Antonescu's torturers. This report will seem quite likely to those who remember the mass suicides among Viennese Jews after the Anschluss. It indicates what the British government is prepared to do to fugitive workers from fascist tyranny; what the 'war for freedom' really amounts to. Anarchists can show no surprise at this; they have been exposing the nature of governments for decades.

The left press has hardly raised its voice about the 'Struma' tragedy — the *New Statesman and Nation* gave a lukewarm account of it at the end of its editorial recently. We are not surprised that the social chauvinists lay no stress on this instance of the hollowness of British war aims. Their support for the authority which committed this crime, whose hands are stained with the blood of these 769 Jewish refugees, is only one more indication of the 'socialists' treachery to the cause of the international working class which they claim to champion. But the workers should take note of the case of the 'Struma', which shows that the European governments, no less than the South American governments which kept the refugees from Vichy France under the horrible conditions described in the February issue of WAR COMMENTARY ('Hell Ships for Refugees'*), are totally indifferent to the fate of the victims of fascism. Whatever the professions of indignation and horror British politicians continually make in order to spur on the workers to fight for them, these actions clearly show the hollowness and hypocrisy of their pretensions.

mid-March 1942.

* Reprinted in *Neither East Nor West*, page 43 — Editor.

Government and Terrorism
Hypocrisy in Palestine

The blowing up of the King David Hotel on 22nd July has resulted in an enormous spate of sanctimonious horror from official circles in the British Government and also from high-up Jewish and Arab sources. No doubt the blowing up was a horrible business; loss of life is always something which shocks humane feelings. But to raise one's hands in an attitude of pious disapproval is just not enough. These things do not happen without cause; and when one considers the background of such acts of terrorism, the sanctimonious hypocrisy of the Government stands revealed. For, as in all terroristic acts by individuals or illegal organisations, they are a seemingly inevitable outcome of long continued governmental terrorism conducted under the mask of law and order.

Palestine and Imperialism

Both the Jewish and the Arab communities in Palestine resent British rule. The 'disturbances' of 1936 were chiefly the outcome of Arab hostility to the British Mandate; now it is chiefly the Jews. We have shown over and over again in this paper how Imperialism maintains its sway by setting off one section of a community against another. Earlier in the year we published an article showing how the British were deliberately inflaming Arab-Jewish hostility; they have not failed to utilise the Arab casualties in the King David Hotel to further this policy. But it is necessary to recall how the British rule came to be dominant over Palestine in the first place.

In the House of Commons on 19th June 1936, Commander Locker-Lampson declared: "People talk about Palestine as though we wanted it only for the Jews. The truth is that the Mandate is the luckiest thing for the British Empire that has happened, perhaps for a generation. If only we realised that we should try to make it a most essential element in a new strategic movement . . . There is another great highway, the Suez Canal, which has become the true key and pivot of strategic considerations of the future . . . *By conquering Palestine, he (Lord Allenbury) guaranteed security to the Canal.*" This passage indicates not only how Britain acquired Palestine, but also the reasons why Palestine is retained with such tenacity. That these views are not merely Conservative in origin is shown by the unanimously accepted resolutions of the Labour

Party Conference in 1936 supporting the British Mandate on the grounds that "the situation of Palestine makes it a point of extreme strategic importance and as such, an object for rival imperialist ambitions" which should therefore remain under British control!

When these considerations are remembered, the oily talk of the British Administration in Palestine about their duty towards the population, and their determination not to be deterred from carrying out their duties by menaces from terror-groups, etc., becomes simply nauseous in its hypocrisy.

What British rule involves

We have said that terrorism is always born of terroristic government. For years now Palestine has been governed under virtual Martial Law — under the Palestine (Defence) Order in Council, 1937, and recently under the Defence (Emergency) Regulations 1945. These allow of arrest without warrant, and detention without trial. "These two regulations are widely employed", declared the *News Chronicle* of 2nd August. "There are thousands of persons arrested without warrant and imprisoned without trial — although 'imprisonment' is called 'detention'. Detention camps and prisons at Latrun, Rafa, Acre, Haifa and elsewhere are full of them and some have been there three years without charge or trial. Sometimes, when there is sufficient evidence, offenders are brought before the military courts, where their defence is undertaken by an officer appointed by the Court, and can and do receive sentences ranging from a few weeks to life imprisonment or capital punishment."

That can fairly be called legal terrorism. In another country it would be called fascism. But the administration has for years been engaged in systematic terrorism with or without any legal base. The Government imposes 'collective fines' on whole villages "the inhabitants of which *there is reason to believe* have committed or connived at crimes or acts of lawlessness". It also demolishes without compensation houses where crimes are supposed to have been committed or abetted. Several hundreds of houses in Jaffa alone have been blown up under this Order. Letters, telegrams, and the press are subject to censorship, and the whole method of government is indistinguishable from fascism.

The villagers of Al Tirah described in a petition events which took place there on 4th June 1936: "The soldiers entered houses, collected what they could of food, clothes and furniture and set it on fire . . . The owners, who watched helplessly, were beaten or struck down with the butts of rifles." In the end no arms were found, in spite of threats, and the soldiers left having destroyed everything but the money of the villagers, which they took with them. In another village (Al Taibah) 159 men were rounded up and forced to march all day. Those who became tired were beaten and two who attempted to escape were shot down. One was bludgeoned with a rifle butt as he lay wounded, and both died in hospital. Many similar cases are known of brutality and murder." (Quoted from *Spain and the World*, 29th July 1938)

Such incidents are being repeated now; the *News Chronicle's* Special Correspondent Geoffrey Hoare wrote (2nd August): "There has been an outcry in the local press against 'Jews being knocked about or beaten at Talbieh Military Detention Barracks (where the curfew-breakers are taken)' and being roughly handled when picked up in the streets. Many of these complaints have been legally sworn to, as have some regarding what is euphemistically called 'horseplay', when troops shouting 'King David' are alleged to have beaten prisoners and then forced them to shout in chorus: 'The English are good'. This behaviour is so reminiscent of Nazi Jew-baiting that it is unnecessary to stress it.

Callousness to Immigrants

The Zionist politicians press for increased Jewish immigration into Palestine because they want to set up their own state, and advance their own political interests. The British attitude is influenced primarily by British Imperial interests in Palestine (salts and oil-pipeline, etc.), and secondarily by its 'Divide and Rule' tactics; but the suffering involved in such opposition to Zionist political aims is not felt by the Zionists, but by the wretched Jewish refugees and displaced persons who form the cargoes of the refugee ships.

During the war, the British turned back shiploads of Jewish refugees who had escaped from occupied Europe. They therefore condemned them to death at the hands of the Nazi authorities from whom they had escaped, or to suicide as a result of despair. In at least one case such a ship sank with all aboard. Much the same kind of thing is still happening. "Tomorrow morning sick and pregnant women amongst nearly 6,000 illegal immigrants in Haifa Harbour will be brought ashore and taken to Athlit clearance camp. *It is feared that if the Government, as they have every right to do, deported them, there would be a wave of suicides, especially among the pregnant women who form part of all illegal shiploads.*"

(*News Chronicle*, 2nd August 1946) Let us say right away that we do not recognise the 'right' of a Government to take actions which drive its victims to suicide.

Hostile population

This is the kind of brutality and violence which the British have been carrying on in Palestine for years. Whatever the attitude of the population as a whole towards the 'terrorists' it is inevitable that they refuse to assist the police of the Mandatory tyranny to run them to earth. Just how oppressive is police rule was demonstrated by the thoroughness with which the British carried out the round-up in Tel Aviv in which every house was entered and British doctors were even on hand to examine invalids and see if they were 'really' ill! (Such action would constitute assault in this country.)

General Baker's anti-Semitic declaration, imposing a non-fraternisation order, and urging British troops and civilians to "hit the Jew where he feels it most — in his pocket" is hardly different from the kind of thing for which the Attorney General has just denounced the Nazi high-ups at Nuremburg. Yet the Government has not repudiated General Baker's speech. It would be difficult to imagine anything less calculated to promote peaceful relations in Palestine.

What is the 'solution'?

Any attempt to solve the Palestine question must keep in mind the fundamentally incompatible factors involved. The clash of Imperialisms; the determination of Britain to hold on to assets in Palestine, and guard Imperial lifelines; the political ambitions of Zionist Jewish Nationalism and the rival ambitions of Arab politicians in Arab Nationalism; the setting-off of these two against each other by the British and their willingness to be used in this way which hinders the mutual solidarity of Jewish and Arab workers. 'Realist' political theorists try and suggest 'compromises' which they advance as 'solutions'. When 'utopians' like the anarchists say that there is no solution within those terms of reference, and therefore it is necessary radically to alter the whole framework of Palestine affairs before any solution can be reached — we are told that we are hopelessly 'unrealistic'. But it is clear that in fact our position is far more realistic than all these 'Palestine Plans' and partitions and compromises which in reality only serve as a cover for the continued predominance of British

Imperialism, and the schemes of other Imperialist powers to share in the gains of Palestine.

Men and women in Palestine will never be free and materially secure while Imperial domination lasts. They will not secure freedom by exchanging the British Mandate for rule of Jewish capitalists and landlords or Arab capitalists and landlords. There is no solution through the triumph of one or other of the conflicting Nationalisms. Since the organised resistance in Palestine is clearly under the control of Jewish nationalists, it receives no support from us, though we do not for that reason join the chorus of sanctimonious protest set up by the British fascists. Our sympathies lie with the common people, Jewish or Arab, who suffer under whatever government is imposed upon them, and whose blood is shed either in mistaken adherence to their nationalist pretensions or in blind reprisals against such action.

Peace will come to Palestine only when all existing ruling groups, and all would-be rulers are rendered powerless and impotent by the land and the instruments of production passing under the direct control of the workers — Jewish and Arab — themselves, without any tutelage from above. The internal problems of Palestine can only be solved by the social revolution; while the elimination of the external factors or rival imperialisms also awaits the social revolution in the countries involved. Until that time comes the rule of bloodshed and brutality which is Imperialism will continue to shock the conscience of humane people all over the world. Such people should join their efforts to the cause and ideals of the revolution.

10th August 1946

Quit Palestine Now!

Anti-Semitic Demonstrations are Debasing and Futile

The hanging of the two British sergeants kidnapped by Jewish terrorists is undoubtedly a horrible incident, but it is only an *incident* in the history of bloodshed that has marked British rule in Palestine during the past twenty-five years. Terrorism in Palestine has not been the exclusive weapon of the Jews. For many years before the war it was the Arabs. And the methods used by the British administration throughout can only be described as governmental terrorism.

But the National Press whose spokesmen have been attacking the Government over the newsprint cut on the grounds that it represents an attack on the Freedom of the Press have, nevertheless, found all the necessary space to splash the Sergeant's case over the front pages of their papers. In the case of the evening papers of Wednesday July 30th, the announcement that the two sergeants had been "found Roped to Trees" was headlined, though later that same evening it was announced in the 9 o'clock news by the BBC that in fact they had not yet been found! It was only the following morning that the bodies were found.

We mention this as one example of the irresponsibility of the Press in this country in connection with events in Palestine. But the main charge to be levelled at the National Press is the eagerness of certain papers to give undue prominence to this case, knowing that it was bound to have unpleasant repercussions in the country. We do not suggest that the incident should have been suppressed, but that it should not have been presented in such a way as to be used as an excuse for anti-semitic demonstrations. Incidents have already been reported in Glasgow and Liverpool where Jewish shops have been stoned, fired and looted. In Manchester a crowd of civilians and soldiers started a demonstration in the Jewish quarter which was preceded by window-smashings in various parts of the city and as we go to press an anti-Jewish demonstration has taken place in London, and stone-throwing damaged six windows of a synagogue at Catford Hill. It is not the material damage to property with which we are here concerned but with the mentality of the people who take part in these demonstrations. That latent anti-semitism exists in this country must be admitted with a feeling of shame. The editors of the sensational press must be aware and some even responsible for this, and in presenting the news of the sergeants in the way they did, they are guilty of inciting hooligan elements to take part in anti-semitic demonstrations. Not one of these papers has so far attempted to show that the Jews in this country cannot in any way be held responsible for what is happening in Palestine, and no appeal has yet been published to restrain people from excesses such as in Liverpool, Glasgow and Manchester.

Our voice is a small one by comparison, but at least we know that the anarchists will be using all their powers of persuasion to stop people from joining in vocal as well as physical anti-semitic demonstrations.

Terrorism Breeds Terrorism

A year ago we published an editorial on this page in connection with the blowing up of the King David Hotel (*Freedom* 10th August 1946) in which we pointed out that "No doubt the blowing up was a horrible business; loss of life is always something which shocks humane feelings. But to raise one's hands in an attitude of pious disapproval is just not enough. These things do not happen without cause; and when one considers the background of such acts of terrorism, the sanctimonious hypocrisy of the Government stands revealed. For, as in all terroristic acts by individuals or illegal organisations they are a seemingly inevitable outcome of long continued governmental terrorism conducted under the mask of law and order." The argument we used a year ago to explain the King David explosion applies equally well to-day in the case of the two sergeants.

This year nine Jewish 'terrorists' have been sentenced to death by the British. Seven were hanged and two committed suicide on the eve of their execution. None of these men so far as we can ascertain were charged with being responsible for the death of a British soldier. Three were condemned to death by a military court for their part in the attack on Acre gaol where hundreds of Jews are being held, without trial, simply as suspected 'terrorists'. They were successful in the attempt to release their comrades and presumably this is the 'crime' which earned them the British hangman's rope.

In Palestine to-day the death sentence can be passed on Jews caught carrying arms. Presumably, the anti-semitic demonstrators of Liverpool will answer that drastic measures must be taken, and it is only by threatening the big stick that terrorism in Palestine will be stamped out. But, in fact, increased governmental terrorism will only meet with more terrorism from individuals and illegal organisations.

How Will It End?

The British Government has hanged nine 'terrorists'. The terrorists have hanged two British sergeants and threaten to hang another seven. The British troops in avenging the death of their two comrades kill five Jewish civilians in Tel-Aviv. A further 23 Jews were injured the following day during the funeral procession for the five victims. Now Hagana (the Jewish organisation whose co-operation the British have been seeking in their anti-terrorist campaign) retaliates by threatening "reprisals against troops and police 'who kill and injure innocent Jews in revenge for the murder of the two sergeants'." How will it all end? At the moment it is clear that terrorism will be answered with terrorism. The Jewish terrorists (as, incidentally, the Arab terrorists earlier) have shown their determination in a way that must convince the British that intimidation, threats and even the hangman's rope will not succeed in stamping them out. Their sang froid and skill (which many of them learned in the British commandos fighting for 'democracy'!) cannot be denied, and their fanatical nationalism a continued British administration in Palestine will only intensify.

Is there a solution to the 'Palestine question'? As we have pointed out on other occasions, in discussing this question the fundamentally incompatible factors involved must be kept in mind. The clash of Imperialism; the determination of Britain to hold on to assets in Palestine, and guard Imperial lifelines; the political ambitions of Zionist Jewish Nationalism, and the rival ambitions of Arab politicians in Arab Nationalism; the setting-off of these two against each other by the British, and their willingness to be used in this way hinders the mutual solidarity of Jewish and Arab workers. 'Realist' political theorists try and suggest 'compromises' which they advance as 'solutions'. When 'utopians' like the anarchists say that there is no solution within those terms of reference, and therefore it is necessary radically to alter the whole framework of Palestine affairs before any solution can be reached — we are told that we are hopelessly 'unrealistic'. But it is clear that in fact our position is far more realistic than all these 'Palestine Plans' and partitions and compromises which in reality only serve as a cover for the continued predominance of British Imperialism, and the schemes of other Imperialist powers to share in the gains of Palestine.

Withdraw British Troops
The first step in solving the Palestine question must be the complete and immediate withdrawal of British troops from that country.

Let not the part-time 'humanitarians' raise their hands in horror and cry "If we leave Palestine there will be terrible bloodshed". That argument has been used as an excuse to maintain British rule in India during the past 150 years, and yet the British are now having to leave, bloodshed or no bloodshed. This hypocritical argument must not be allowed to prevail as a justification for keeping troops in Palestine for years to come.

If those misguided hooligans who have been 'avenging' the two British sergeants by smashing up Jewish shops and stoning synagogues are genuinely shocked by what is happening in Palestine and are anxious to stop such things happening on a much larger scale, they would do well to use up their energies by walking through the streets with placards marked *"British Must Quit Palestine Now"*. At least they will be showing some practical understanding whereas their present actions can only come under the heading of 'attempted terrorism'.
9th August 1947

Political Background in Palestine

(From our Middle East Correspondent)

The reason so many people fail to understand the Palestine situation is because they think exclusively in nationalist terms. Hence they look with optimism or pessimism at this or that latest Conference or Commission that is going to settle the problem once and for all, and never think that the very political existence of nationalist politicians means that some problem or another has to be kept alive. Partition is an old-established way of doing that. Whereas, from an anarchist point of view, what is a preliminary to a rational approach to the problem is the complete abandonment of nationalism. This may be 'utopian' but it is not as hopeless as trying to reconcile 'Arabs' and 'Jews', particularly when one realises that not only are the 'official' viewpoints classified under those headings quite irreconcilable, but Arabs no more wholly accept the 'Arab case' and Jews the 'Jewish case' than everyone in Britain accept the wishy-washy liberalism expounded over the BBC.

The Jewish Attitude
For instance, most Jews in Palestine support the illegal army, the Haganah, and oppose the terrorists, while the left-wing and right-wing divide on the question of a bi-national or a Jewish

national State. Many do not favour independent statehood at all, and advocate British Imperialism, federation with neighbouring Arab states or other solutions. The majority of Jews outside Palestine are not Zionists at all; while the majority of Zionists outside Palestine are opposed or lukewarm to the Haganah and favour the Irgun and occasionally the Sternists.

The Arab Attitude

As regards the Arabs there are two divergent points of view in the main: the conciliationists such as Abdel Rahman Azzan Pasha, Secretary of the Arab League who is not only not hostile to the Jews, but is also prepared to meet with the Zionists to the point of agreeing to a Jewish minority in an Arab Palestine (i.e. a Zionist 'National Home' as a minority) and the extremists such as Fawzi Kawukji whose sole aim is to drive the Jews right out of Palestine.

Not only that, but it may also be pointed out that the alleged solid front of Arabs supporting the 'Palestine Arab case' are not quite able to meet in perfect harmony. For if King Ibn Saud, Lord of Hejaz and King of Saudi Arabia, and foremost champion of Moslem Palestine, met Fawzi Kawukji, leader of the illegal Arab Army devoted to the Mufti of Jerusalem, he would probably cut his head off! Kawukji is not only wanted by the Palestine Police; he was also under sentence of death in Syria but escaped from the French a few hours ahead of the firing squad. He joined King Feisal in Iraq and was banished for conspiring against the throne, and became Ibn Saud's military adviser until he organised the Pan-Arab revolt of Ibn Rafadi of the Billis tribe from Saudi Arabia to Transjordan. Ibn Saud swore to cut his head off personally, and Kawukji went to Transjordan where he began organising a new Arab Army, and was the leader of the Arab rebellion in 1936, holding Northern Palestine and defying even the RAF. His guerilla tactics were remarkable and terrifying, and need to be recalled to-day when the initiative in terrorism has passed to the Jews, since Kawukji is now on the hilly frontier of Palestine awaiting the hour to move back. What a terrible civil war there is going to be in Palestine when rival terrorists meet!

Choosing the Lesser Evil

How far there will be an unbroken front on either side is hard to prophesy. Ibn Saud would like to see an Arab State in Palestine but my humble guess is that he would sooner see Dr Weizmann crowned King of Jerusalem than see Fawzi Kawukji get near to his goal of Pan-Arabia under his own leadership. And it is doubtful whether Abdullah of Transjordan, who is anxious enough about Zionist claims to Transjordan as well as Palestine, would like to see Kawukji strong on his borders. He may well be prepared to see his army defeated by the Jews in spite of his support for this same army of the Mufti. Hence the Rahman Pasha plan for an Arab Palestine with a strong Jewish minority — just strong enough to curb any potential Arab ruler — may well suit the Arab Kings and Rulers, none of whom like to see each other too strong and all of whom have ambitions that are bound to clash.

This does not alter the fact that a very bloody civil war can result in Palestine, the illegal Arab and Jewish armies, of which there are more than one on each side, being versed in guerilla tactics. The only alternative is the faint possibility of a non-nationalist body of sentiment on either side, causing a different outlook altogether. But this presupposes a great deal more social revolutionary feeling than actually exists.

One thing is certain. If British troops are used in this struggle — and they undoubtedly will be — it will be for the furtherance of what Whitehall considers are 'our' interests since there is nobody in Palestine other than those admittedly believing in British Imperialism who wants to see British troops there. The lives that are lost as a result of Army intervention will not be for the protection of anything but Mr Bevin's reputation for being firm.
9th August 1947   A. M.

Palestine 1948

The rattle of machine-guns echoes through the streets of Jerusalem and Jaffa. Bombs explode, and men die. Throughout the Middle East, troops assemble and arm. The American, Russian, British and French governments all seek to exploit, as far as their divergent imperialist interests will permit, the Jewish-Arab conflict which they have done so much to provoke. But no-one seems to be able to understand what it is all about — not even those who are killing, or being killed. It seems to be essential that

we should put before our readers certain basic truths on the social
background of the Palestine struggle.

What we are reading in the left-wing press on this subject is
nothing but propaganda in the worst sense of the word —
emotional word-spinning on purely sentimental predilections with
not the slightest effort to analyse the facts. Many among them are
pro-Zionist because they are aware of the sufferings endured by
the Jewish *Diaspora*, the Western Jewish populations, during the
war; or because they have read of the agrarian co-operative
colonies in Palestine. The others are pro-Arab because of their
attachment to the idea of the emancipation of colonial people and
their hatred of capitalist intrusions.

The actual problem is far less simple, and cannot be decided by
ethnological sympathies or communal ties. Palestine is in a vital
strategic position for the control of the Arabian peninsula, of the
Eastern Mediterranean, and the Suez Canal. It is a market for
British, American and Arab traders. It is a battleground between
two imperialist blocs seeking raw materials; between two social
theories, statism and liberalism; between two economic systems,
Jewish capitalism and Arab feudalism. It is also a mosaic of
'minorities', racial and religious; and a land of social experiments.
For the Zionist Jew it is the promised national home, for the Arab
nationalist it is a land to be liberated from the infidel.

National Frontiers and Class Frontiers

On the other hand, each of these factors has many aspects.
Although certain general tendencies characterise the Jewish and
Arab movements, their component elements are of great variety.
It is not a political colour, but an economic one which disturbs the
rainbow of opinions which the Jewish Agency and the Arab High
Commission claim to represent.

There is, without doubt, less irreconcilability between certain
Zionist and Arab elements (for example that of the rector of the
Hebrew University of Jerusalem, Lieb Magnes, and that of the
Ittihad group — both factions favouring Jewish-Arab co-
operation), than between the ultra-nationalists faithful to the
fascist conceptions of their dead leader Jabotinsky and the
supporters of the Left Socialist organisation *Paole Zion*, or
between certain Arab workers' unions and the great feudal
Moslem chiefs.

In 1945 and 1946 lightning strikes united Jewish and Arab
workers in a common struggle against the British mandatory

authorities and against certain employers. Some quarters, for example, of the station area of Tel Aviv, are inhabited by a mixed population of poor workers. The similarity of their conditions of life has brought about active co-operation which is re-inforced by a common dislike of the British authorities. But, these partial and limited tendencies towards communal harmony are not at present sufficient to counter-balance the great ethnic, religious, and economic forces of the two opposing civilisations.

The West Invades the East
The Jews represent the West, its technique, its enterprising spirit, its organising ability. Although there are thousands of Eastern Sephardic Jews, the recent immigrants form the majority. The dynamic of Zionist life is found in the stream of capital and personnel from the *Diaspora* — the Jewish communities scattered throughout the world, to the *Yishuv* — the Jews of Palestine. The Jewish Agency, the actual Zionist government, co-ordinates, harmonises, and reconciles opposing tendencies.

The immigrants have brought with them bold projects and thorough experience of industry and commerce. They have set up new enterprises and helped to transform the country into an economic centre capable of satisfying many of the needs of the Near East and Middle East markets.

The *Histradout*, the Jewish General Federation of Labour, besides being a trade union, is an immense production co-operative which carries out contracts for big public works, not only for the Palestine government, but also for the British authorities. This organisation has built great strategic roads and military installations for the British, not only in Palestine, but in the Lebanon and Syria.

Finally, there are the agricultural pioneers of the *Kibbutzim*, following their religious, political, or social affinities, continually penetrating further into the interior of the country. Some of them are organised on a basis of absolute equality, following strictly socialist methods and principles. Money is not used within the community, equality of the sexes is a reality, all administrative powers are purely functional and executive. State farms and Collective farms of the Soviet type are considered by many of these pioneers to be an obsolete organisational form, vitiated by the Statist principle.

But, behind this liberty and this disinterestedness, there remains all the same, the power of money.

The Basis of the Question
In effect, it is financial assistance, mainly from North America,
which keeps these enterprises going, more like voluntary labour
camps or the outposts of political infiltration, than genuine
economic experiments. It is not difficult to understand the
solidarity that exists between the Zionist colonies, the Jewish
Agency and the *Diaspora*. Solidarity of race, and of interests,
appears everywhere, in organisation, in external propaganda, and
in the Defence Army, but above all in the distribution of the
Manna from Heaven — the providential dollar.

Reduced to defending themselves in the coastal towns, the
Jewish bourgeoisie could not hold out for long in the event of an
Arab uprising. Deprived of the umbilical cord which has continued
to nourish them since birth — the pious gifts of the whole world —
the *Kibbutzim* would disappear at the first general Moslem
uprising. The youth of the agricultural colonies are active,
well-trained and audacious, their type changes more and more in
every generation from that of the traditional Jew of the Ghetto to
that of an occupying army. They provide the finest troops of the
Haganah, and the most active groups of the *Irgun*. Zionism is still
in the stage of conquest, in the political-military phase.

This situation is not without its advantages — it saves the
occupied as well as the occupiers from the most ruthless aspects of
'primitive accumulation'. But it makes no clearer the social
problem which is still veiled by its secondary aspects. It would be
necessary no doubt for the country to reach its demographic
saturation, its maximum population density in relation to its
productive capacity, for the class tendencies to show themselves
clearly, disrupting the apparent national unity, born of the
colonising spirit and cemented by ethnological ties.

Economic Weakness of the Arab World
On the other side we find a feudal economy, incapable of
competing with any hope of success against the Zionist assault.
The rich Arab is a landowner, a trader or speculator, rarely an
industrialist. His religious and caste traditions are the reason for
this. He looks with envy upon the success of the newcomers to
Palestine. After having sold his reputedly desert lands to Jewish
buyers, he finds that 'Western Methods' have rendered them
fertile and productive. The reaction has been an anti-Zionist
movement in the political field, the diversion of social discontent
into anti-Jewish channels, attempts to create new Arab industry in

the economic field, efforts to supplant the Jewish colonies but to make use of their technical and financial innovations.

Serious obstacles impede the following of this last aim which presupposes the rupture of the Zionist umbilical cord. Apart from the managerial inferiority of the Arabs, the most important is the extremely low purchasing power of the Arab masses. Another is the traditional mistrust of the wealthy Arabs, of placing their capital in industrial enterprises.

An example of the divergent tendencies of Zionist and Arab commercial activities was given by the visit of their two commercial delegations to London. The Jewish delegation negotiated for the purchase of machinery and raw materials; the Arab envoys sought finished goods, less costly and more immediately saleable.

To sum up, Palestine is a country where the capitalist and industrial forms of national independence *have not yet been achieved*, either by the Arabs or the Jews. Perhaps it should be added that *they no longer can be*, in a world dominated by two great imperialisms.

Conclusions

The solution of the Palestine problem will only be found outside the sphere of national states, and outside the capitalist system. But is this not also the case in all countries, is it not the case throughout Europe? What do the phrases 'National independence' and 'capitalist prosperity' mean to-day? Nothing, absolutely nothing.

We hope that the Jewish and Arab people, like those of all countries, will learn this from the inextricable difficulties into which they have been thrown by their ambitious and ruthless masters.

24th January 1948   DAMASHKI

A STATE IS BORN

3

Israel — A New State

(From a Middle East Correspondent)

With the ending of the British Mandate in Palestine comes the declaration of a Jewish State, to be known as Israel. The new State adopts intact the laws left by the old administration, with the exception of the control of immigration set out in the White Paper of 1939. It struggles to achieve national sovereignty, it transforms the Haganah into an Army, it legalises its own police, it has an organised religion to form an 'Established Church' — in fact, none of the ingredients of Statehood are missing. All one can ask is what advance does this represent?

Those who now pin their illusions on this newest amongst the States will, if they survive the present conflict, live to see yet a fresh illusion smashed. The survivors of the Irish 1916 rebellion who later declared with joy the establishment of the State later known as Eire, saw the steady decline of the dream of an Irish Republic. The Italians who fought with Garibaldi to form an Italian Republic saw — some of them its steady decline through monarchy to fascism. Nationalism and Statehood have never brought freedom. If any gleam of hope has ever been seen amongst the Zionist experiment, it was the fact that many colonists were able in their early days of struggle to dispense with the State and live their life without reliance on any central authority until their nationalism or religion got the better of their natural instincts.

There is only one difference between this national revolution and any others. The State of Israel proclaimed for the first time since Old Testament days cannot claim that all are present or that it has the support of any Jews other than "the Jewish people in Palestine and the *Zionist* movement of the world" as its inaugural proclamation stated, thus admitting to 'the lost tribes of Israel', namely the non-Zionist Jews throughout the world, most of whom (possibly the majority of Jews) are completely assimilated save for religious customs they may or may not observe, and the clearest thinkers of whom are completely internationalist in their outlook.

Latest Socialist Premier

The Government set up in Israel is a victory for the social-democratic movement, whose stock was thought to be declining. The key posts are all in Socialist hands, and David Ben-Gurion becomes the latest Socialist Premier. The President is Dr Weizmann, who, although not a Labour Party man himself, does in fact register a big victory for their policy in view of the hatred felt for him by the Jewish Fascist Party (IZL) as well as the opposition to him by the Revisionists and orthodox religious parties, in fact by all who supported either the American or Russian dominance and opposed Dr Weizmann's consistently pro-British policy, which is the line of the Labour Party and Labour Federation as well as of the Haganah which now becomes the official Jewish Army.

Forgotten Men

The Arabs have not declared a Government; they are in fact the forgotten men of Palestine, and nobody at present even pretends to represent them. The foreign Arab armies are doing that for them. The complete collapse of the Palestine Arabs is due to various reasons. The Mufti was foisted on to them by the Arab Higher Committee which was as obsessed by his 'great name' as the British Conservative Party was by Churchill's in 1945. In fact, the feudal Husseini family is not popular, and the Mufti's pro-Nazi support during the war lost him most of the support he had before it; also he could not stand up to the rival claims of men like Abdullah. No Palestine Arab dared to oppose him openly before the fighting began, but when it started his name was not sufficient to evoke support. The military hope of the Palestine Arabs was Fawzi Kawukji — a noted terrorist — but conditions now are open warfare and he failed as a soldier. Moreover he, more than any other leading Palestine Arab, is hated by the other Arab kings and rulers.

Many Palestine Arabs feel that whoever wins, they lose, and this may explain the frenzied rush to leave Haifa to the Jews, get out of Jaffa at any price, and to surrender Acre while new rifles were left unpacked. These places were defended by Palestine Arabs. The only advances made have been by the invading Arab armies, amongst which only the British officered, British supplied and British trained army of Transjordan has made any show. King Abdullah is Whitehall's own little king. What game Mr Bevin is playing with Abdullah is not yet known. It may be that he hopes to enforce partition between puppet King Abdullah, who will be pro-British (or else!) and pro-British Jewish leaders such as Weizmann and Ben-Gurion. Thus, whoever wins, the Foreign Office has won. But this is a dangerous game as it may mean the coming to power of the Jewish Fascist movement (IZL) which would just as soon have relations with Russia. Hence Truman's immediate rush to recognise Israel before Russia had a chance to, and one of the reasons (other than Zionist electoral pressure) why he will keep on more or less supporting the Zionists, but not so much as to alienate the Arab rulers on whom American capitalism depends for oil.

Sitting on a Volcano

The Arab countries, other than Transjordan, have not distinguished themselves in the invasion. None of the governments really welcomed this war, but they were too committed to it to back out, and further, they did not dare face popular repercussions at home where the war is popular because it is against 'the foreigner', and in an Arab attack on the Jews the man in the street can visualise an attack on the British, the Americans, the Russians and more particularly Greeks and Armenians and every other well-to-do foreigner in Alexandria and Cairo. Basically they think of it as a war against the West. War does not strike them as particularly tragic, since World War II brought nothing but high wages in military establishments, plentiful work, and a big influx of soldiers and a stimulus to trade. Nobody in the Arab world has any idea of war, other than the completely uninfluential people who inhabited the desert in which World Wars I and II were conveniently fought out. But a long war would bring disillusion, bitterness, and bring to a head the long smouldering discontent of the fellaheen against the Governments and the 'effendin', for which anti-foreignism is only a temporary substitute.

Hope for the Future

On the Jewish side a long war would have the reverse effect; it would strengthen the reactionaries by the continual appeal to nationalism, and also the fact that anti-British sentiment arising out of the subsidy to Transjordan would be grist to the mill of the Right. The Socialists are far less rigidly nationalistic and amongst them and in some of the left groupings, there is much more intelligent understanding of the Arab position, and also of the whole question of national sovereignty and statehood. If the totalitarian state did not triumph, they might in later years have some considerable significance. The League for Arab-Jewish rapprochement may have difficulty in functioning but it ha. pioneered this idea of a libertarian approach.

There are in fact three different aspects of hope for the future. One, the possibility of revolutionary discontent in the Arab countries arising out of war causing the reactionary governments to overtopple. Two, the rejection of the idea of national sovereignty by some Arabs and Jews who have an intelligent idea of how to live together although for the moment they are silenced. Three, the fact that the Jewish people outside Palestine have, except for the Zionists, rejected the idea that the state of Israel belongs to them (the Jewish Socialist Bund, influential in many countries, has rejected the idea of Zionism altogether). So, in spite of the weariness yet one more war induces, at least some hope for internationalist principles may be held in this case.

29th May 1948

Assassination and Terror

The assassination of Count Bernadotte has let loose a flood of hysteria and hypocritical outpourings — as is only to be expected from politicians and journalists. It is a distasteful and unfortunate business, the more so because of the personal qualities of the victim, for Count Bernadotte appears to have been well enough aware of the dangers of his position — indeed, his car had already been sniped at earlier on the day of his death — and he had refused to take special precautions. For it is evident that he and his convoy were substantially unarmed, and that the killing was an easy business quite different from the attempts made on the lives of dictators heavily protected by bodyguards and police.

From almost any point of view this assassination appears most untimely. Bernadotte had no physical power; the politicians of the United Nations were aware that his was a dangerous assignment, but they, who do have power to shape the fortunes of the people living in Palestine, sit safe and unharmed, singing requiems for Bernadotte. It is practically certain that for many political interests the assassination will be regarded as a godsend, whatever they may say in telegrams of condolence to the widow. For obviously the wave of anti-Jewish sentiment can be exploited to the full. As always in the world of politics reactions of sincerity have no place, and practical considerations will ensure that capital be made out of any event however much of personal tragedy it contains.

Complexity of Motive and Effect

Assassination is a complex business and it is idiotic to take a 'simple' view of it. We have said that Bernadotte had no power — he was merely there to administer the truce. But even this is only a half-truth, for as the representative of the United Nations there loomed behind him all the powers of the imperialist governments restrained only by the conflicts of their various interests. From a certain point of view Bernadotte's very qualities thus made him a more effective instrument in the hands of an imperialist international organisation. Such is always the fate of sincere and honest individuals who interfere in politics: their good qualities are used to cover up the sordid intrigues that are the soul of politics. They should resist the flattery which seeks to prostitute their honesty and good will.

Inevitably the press as a whole has been content to express 'horror and indignation' (do journalists and press lords know the meaning of such feelings?) rather than to seek causes. An exception must be made of Arthur Koestler's dispatch to the *Manchester Guardian* on the morrow of the murder. While unreservedly condemning the act, Koestler is careful to point out that terrorism has its historical causes. "The terrorist underground struggle against the hostile mandatory power conformed", he wrote, "whatever one's opinion about the rights and wrongs of the case, to a classic historical pattern". He goes on to denounce the present case as different in kind from the use of violence against the occupying British Army in the past, but he retains a sense of historical proportion: "After the first horror and indignation is past one further consideration is important. Even the worst outrage has its social causes. The only sincere way for the United Nations to honour the memory of Count Bernadotte is to abolish

the evil which lies at the root of the tragedy. The disastrous and
unnatural situation (in Palestine) must be brought to a speedy
end." We do not share Koestler's political standpoint, nor his
perpetual search for sincerity in politics, but we welcome his
method and his levelheadedness. The roots of so-called terrorism
(it is the name used by far more terroristic governments) make an
intensely interesting study, only to be understood by a careful
historical examination of past instances.

The Israeli State
Meanwhile, what of the Palestinian government? The present
event shows it conforming to the familiar pattern of power
institutions. In the past the militant political movement of Zionism
had shown itself ready enough to profit from individual acts of
violence which advanced its aims. Now that they are in power, the
terrorists who helped them there have become an embarrassment
— 'They must be rooted out!' And immediately one sees that even
this immature, newly-fledged state has all the attributes of such an
instrument of ruling power — army, police, courts, prisons,
judges, and a priesthood to utter the moral exhortations and
'cover' suitable to the ruling sections — they are all there, like ugly
cuckoos elbowing social justice out.

For the Jewish world also has its Bernadottes and General
Councils. Behind the sincere fighters for the rights of the Jews,
those who have struggled against anti-Semitism and the oppression
of minorities, stand the Nationalists, figures not without their
attraction during their years of struggle, but showing all the
familiar vices and insincerities of politics when they attain to
power. The peoples of the world have the examples of Ireland and
of India — to name only instances within the British Empire —
and they now see the same thing happening in Israel. There is
bitter truth in the cynical saying the only lesson of history is that
people do not learn from history.
2nd October 1948

Palestine

The war in Palestine continues to take up headlines in the Press, as politicians bicker in pretences at armistices and parleys, not in the least in an endeavour to find a reasonable solution, but solely in order to preserve the balance of power existing in the 'cold war'.

The ironic nature of the war is that the opposing forces consider themselves as fighting against something which does not happen to be on the other side of the barricades. The thousands of immigrants arriving from Europe are passionately keen to defend their stakes in Israel, and after years in DP camps and concentration camps they are anxious to 'fight back'; but, of course, the Arabs they are fighting against were not responsible for European anti-Semitism. The Arabs regard themselves as fighting against European influence; to them it is a 'new aggression of the West against the East' and they regard it on a par with British Imperialism or the Italian war in Abyssinia.

There is a certain amount of truth in both claims, because undoubtedly much of the outside criticism of Zionism comes from anti-Semitism and support for Zionism out of sympathy with Jewish victims of Nazi and other oppression in Europe. On the other hand, there is no doubt that the majority of Zionists regard the Arabs in the same way as other colonisers have regarded other 'native inhabitants', and it is hardly an answer for the Israeli authorities to claim co-operation from certain Arab tribes, such as the Druses, who have always been on unfriendly terms with other Arabs and inclined towards their enemies. Similar tactics were pursued by the British in India.

There is not the slightest question of Jewish superiority in any renewed outbreak of fighting, no matter how rated the Arab troops may have been in the past; and particularly since the British withdrawal enabled them to bring in thousands of Jewish DP's and also munitions from all over Europe, as well as volunteers. The Arabs accuse Britain of betraying their interests in withdrawing at the particular time it did (had it withdrawn in 1936, for instance, the Jews could have been militarily defeated by them, since at that time they had no possibility of calling in large-scale immigration from Europe, importing arms from countries like Czechoslovakia, nor had they the thousands of British-trained troops from the war.) On the other hand, the Zionists generally have portrayed Britain as aiding the Arabs on the grounds of the association with

Abdullah of Transjordan, and there is a left-wing picture (which is now accepted as truth by all Zionists) of Bevin forcing through a pro-Arab policy against the Cabinet's wish, and being able to call the war off any time he chose.

Bevin's ability to control the Arab States' policy in regard to Palestine (but not in regard to Egypt or the Sudan!) may be doubted. It is more certain that Britain has played a diplomatic game of keeping in with both sides: influencing the Arab countries by the military missions under Glubb, etc., and relying on the pro-British sentiments of Weizmann and the Social-Democrats on the Jewish side. An alternative theory is pointed out by many: namely, that Britain and America — who are agreed on policy in every country in the world — may be not so much at loggerheads over this one small country as may be imagined. America ostensibly and loudly backs the Jewish side and calls on their support in the case of war. This is convenient for whoever may be President (having to placate the New York Jewish vote) and in addition, American influence among European Jewish circles can be considered. On the other hand, Britain ostensibly backs the Arabs — she has 'traditional friendships' among the Arab countries, and calls on their support in the case of war. The Jewish vote in this country does not count very highly, and in any case is not generally pro-Zionist. Thus, whoever wins is an ally against Russia for Britain — or America!

It cannot be doubted that Palestine may be an important focal point in another war, since Russia has seen the weakness of the Arab countries, and that even such a small body as Palestine Jewry can resist them all, and if it had not been restrained, might by now have toppled them all over. Her striking point in a war might well be the oil fields of Iran and with only 'Glubb's Girls' to stop them might soon be in Cairo. The Israeli leaders are well aware of their importance to world politics, and disinclined to give way over limiting their territory, to please the Arabs.

Arab refugees

Meanwhile, the most pressing of all post-war problems has received very little notice — namely the displacement of thousands of Arabs from their homes. These thousands became refugees not because of 'misleading Arab propaganda' as the Israel Government claims, but because they feared terrorists' attacks such as that of the Jewish Fascists on Deir Yassin, when a village which had actually not co-operated with and even resisted Arab terrorists, was massacred by Jewish terrorists. As the thousands of Jewish immigrants come in, the Israel Government can only accommodate them in the deserted Arab cities, and in such towns as Jaffa, transform it completely from an all Arab city to a Jewish city. Before very long, there will simply be nowhere for them to go back to, and having gone, the Israel Government does not particularly want them back, however it condemned the methods which drove them away.

It is futile and unreasonable to blame the Jewish immigrants for this problem of Arab homelessness; they have themselves certainly nowhere else to go, and are naturally bitter at the cynical ease with which Great Powers who deny the great open spaces under their control to settlers, declare that they ought not to go to Palestine but elsewhere. They cannot be expected to stay behind barbed wire and bars until their death, as has been apparently the view of the British Government in its great Cyprus concentration camp experiment (which still goes on). They are no more likely to consider Arab claims than the thousands of Europeans who swarmed to build up America considered the Indians. In spite of all the bunk about peace by settlement and negotiations between the Powers, under the United Nations delusion, the fact is that conflict is in these circumstances inevitable, and victory will certainly go to the strongest side. The Powers are not really interested in any other solution, but are doing their best to use the Palestine struggle as one of the many pawns in the cold war.

No easy solution

As internationalists we ought not to delude ourselves into any other facile solution, but rather to look for hopes that in the future some measure of international co-operation will come about, not between governments or political leaders, but from the people from below, and in the meantime to expose such delusions as those spread by the leaders of all sides in any war. But the major deduction to be drawn from the Palestine conflict is the utter degeneration of Soviet Russia into Czarism, a fact known to anybody with the least perception who witnesses the flight of so many Jews from Europe, but one concealed not least by the Zionist parties who welcome Russian UNO support, and who have in any case a certain vested interest in anti-Semitism. There can be no denying the fact that if conditions were normal and decent in Rumania, Poland, Bulgaria, Czechoslovakia and the other countries behind the Iron Curtain, there would be no 'DP

problem': the fact of open and silent pogroms in those countries
causes the great exodus from Eastern Europe to the overladen DP
camps of Germany and Italy, and the great freights of human
cargo leaving the Danubian ports. The Communists may deny
responsibility for this, but the fact remains that all opposition to
Stalin has been stamped out in those countries and if Stalin so
wished, anti-Semitism could not last a minute. It has not been
tolerated in Russia for many years because of its identification
with and expoitation by the 'White' Czarists, but now that Red
Czarism is so firmly in the saddle, it is used throughout the Great
Russian Empire of Eastern Europe to divide and rule.
27th November 1948   INTERNATIONALIST

Morality in Politics

It was not so long ago that the headlines told us of the gallant
efforts of the illegal Jewish immigrants from Europe to run the
British blockade in Palestine. From a strictly legal point of view
the British were carrying out the policy of limiting immigration to
an agreed figure. The Jews were highly indignant, and there were
some harrowing scenes in the overloaded ships taking them to
Palestine.

One hoped that these experiences would have made them more
understanding towards others in a similar situation. But no,
politicians are all the same whether Jew or Gentile, or Hindu. In
India, Nehru has allowed Gandhi's assassins to be hanged and
admits that thousands of 'Communist suspects' are imprisoned
without trial. His experiences at the hands of British Imperialism
have not taught him anything — except that when one becomes
the ruling class one has to put aside all ideas of justice and
tolerance and follow in the path of one's persecutors.

And now from Israel one learns that in densely populated Arab
villages of Galilee, the Israeli Army is conducting a full-scale
search operation to weed out hundreds of Arab infiltrees from
Lebanon, Syria and Jordan.

In an action completed last month at Shefaram, a large village
north-west of Nazareth, Israeli soldiers collected 200 Arabs who

reportedly had no identification cards. They were transported to the Lebanese frontier and compelled to leave Israel.

The search of Shefaram followed a prescribed pattern. A curfew was imposed on the village and soldiers began a house-to-house check. Those Arabs who had not registered with the military government or who had no cards issued in the last national registration were earmarked for removal.

In October, the Military Governor of Galilee published the warning that local Arabs who aided infiltrees would be fined and imprisoned. Soon afterwards the army moved in and several hundred Arabs were deported.

The Israelis contend that infiltration across wide open frontiers has reached alarming proportions. It is estimated that Israel's Arab population is now above 175,000, an increase of nearly 100,000 in the last year.

A press report states that an Arab Communist member of Israel's Knesset protested against the searches and evictions, describing the operation as 'undemocratic'. Prime Minister David Ben Gurion "turned upon him in full fury" and "accused the Arab legislator of being a former ally of Haj Amin el Husseini, ex-Mufti of Jerusalem and thus a secret agitator against Israel. He asserted that Israel was surrounded by enemies and the infiltration served to undermine the security of the state. In the midst of his angry outburst, he accused the Cominform of 'slandering' the Israel government."

How familiar is this kind of language! When one has no answer one attacks the person or group of persons asking the question, and in working up personal hatred of those people one hopes that the main issue will have been forgotten. How reminiscent of Hitler when he denounced 'International Jewry' or Stalin the 'Trotsky-Fascists'.

Can we learn a lesson from all this? If we do, and act accordingly, then a step has been made towards the realisation of a society without rulers.

24th December 1949   R

4

Postscript:
The New Master Race in Palestine

In these remaining pages we shall concentrate on the Israeli response to the *intifada* over the past 20 months, but in appreciating their role of Master Race over the past 40 years (since the State of Israel was established) Operation 'Peace for Galilee' which was the name given to the invasion of Lebanon in June 1982 cannot be overlooked nor forgotten.

Professor Chomsky has dealt with that campaign (or perhaps 'massacre' would be a more accurate description) in great detail in *The Fateful Triangle*.[1] Two quotations to illustrate the cost in human lives and the utter ruthlessness of the Israeli command. The casualties:

By late June, the Lebanese police gave estimates of about 10,000 killed. These early figures appear to have been roughly accurate. A later accounting reported by the independent Lebanese daily *An-nahar* gave a figure of 17,825 known to have been killed and over 30,000 wounded, including 5,500 killed in Beirut and over 1,200 civilians killed in the Sidon area. A government investigation estimated that 90% of the casualties were civilians. By late December, the Lebanese police estimated the numbers killed through August at 19,085, with 6,775 killed in Beirut, 84% of them civilians. Israel reported 340 IDF [Israel Defence Force] soldiers killed in early September, 446 by late November (if these numbers are accurate, then the number of Israeli soldiers killed in the ten weeks following the departure of the PLO from Lebanon is exactly the same as the number of Israelis killed in all terrorist actions across the northern border from 1967). According to Chief of Staff Eitan, the number of Israeli soldiers killed 'in the entire western sector of Lebanon' — that is, apart from the Syrian front — was 117. Eight Israeli soldiers died 'in Beirut proper', he claimed, three in accidents. If correct (which is unlikely), Eitan's figures mean that five Israeli soldiers were killed in the process of massacring some 6,000 civilians in Beirut, a glorious victory indeed. Israel also offered various figures for casualties within Lebanon. Its final accounting was that 930 people were killed in Beirut including 340 civilians, and that 40 buildings were destroyed in the Beirut bombings, 350 in all of Lebanon. The number of PLO killed was given as 4,000.

As to the methods adopted:

The first target was the Palestinian camp of Rashidiyeh south of Tyre, much of which, by the second day of the invasion, 'had become a field of rubble'. There was ineffectual resistance, but as an officer of the UN peace-keeping force swept aside in the Israeli invasion later remarked: "It was like shooting sparrows with cannon". The 9,000 residents of the camp — which had been regularly bombed and shelled for years from land, sea and air — either fled, or were herded to the beach where they could watch the destruction of much of what remained by the Israeli forces. All teen-age and adult males were blindfolded and bound, and taken to camps, where little has been heard about them since.

   This is typical of what happened throughout southern Lebanon. The Palestinian camps were demolished, largely bulldozed to the ground if not destroyed by bombardment; and the population was dispersed or (in the case of the male population) imprisoned. Reporters were generally not allowed in the Palestinian camps, where the destruction was worst, to keep them from witnessing what had happened and was being done. There were occasional reports. David Shipler described how after the camps were captured the army proceeded to destroy what was left. An army officer, "when asked why bulldozers were knocking down houses in which women and children were living", responded by saying: "they are all terrorists". His statement accurately summarises Israel's strategy and the assumptions that underlie it, over many years.

It is interesting to note that General — as he then was — Sharon justified the massacre in the Lebanon as the way to maintain 'quiet on the West Bank'. How wrong he has proved to be!

   According to *Amnesty International* (June 1989)

On 9 December 1987 demonstrations against the Israeli occupation erupted throughout the West Bank and Gaza, marking the beginning of the period of unrest soon to become known as the *intifada*. Since 9 December almost every day Palestinians, including children, have staged demonstrations in which stones, petrol bombs and other missiles have often been thrown at Israeli soldiers and settlers. The Israeli authorities have responded with force, which has often been excessive and indiscriminate, using such means as live ammunition, rubber and plastic bullets, tear-gas and gravel cannons. More than 360 Palestinians were reported to have been killed by early April 1989 in shooting incidents alone. Thousands have been injured, many of them requiring hospital treatment. A number of Israeli soldiers and civilians too, as well as several Palestinians suspected of collaborating with the Israeli authorities, have been killed in violent attacks by Palestinians.

As well as demonstrations and riots, mass strikes and tax boycotts have been organised by Palestinians in the Occupied Territories, and popular committees have been set up to coordinate such activities and create alternative structures to the Israeli Civil Administration. They have organised, among other things, food distribution, medical relief, and educational programs. Some Palestinian employees of the Israeli Civil Administration, particularly police officials, have resigned from their posts.

In their attempt to suppress such activities, the Israeli authorities resorted to various measures. A number of Palestinian newspapers and institutions were closed down and the popular committees proscribed. Currency restrictions were introduced to control money going to families and institutions in the Occupied Territories. New identity cards were issued in the Gaza Strip to monitor the population more closely. More than 60 Palestinians were served with deportation orders and 48 were actually deported. Villages, towns and refugee camps have been put under prolonged curfew, sometimes for a month or more, during which time electricity, water and telephones have often been disconnected. Trees have been uprooted and crops ruined. Dozens of Palestinian homes have been demolished or sealed up as punishment.

During the first few months of the uprising hundreds of teenagers and young men were arrested, summarily tried on criminal charges — often without legal representation — and sentenced to several months' imprisonment for throwing stones and setting up roadblocks. In March 1988, however, the Israeli authorities decided to make more use of administrative detention. More than 5,000 Palestinians have been in administrative detention since the beginning of the Palestinian *intifada*, most of them for six months; some repeatedly. At least 1,100 are reported to be in detention at present, the vast majority in harsh conditions in the Ketziot detention centre in Israel.

Administrative detention in Israel and the Occupied Territories can and has been abused to detain prisoners of conscience, held for the non-violent exercise of their right to freedom of expression and association.

The International Committee of the Red Cross, one of the few organisations still able to travel relatively freely in the occupied West Bank and Gaza, has accused the Israelis of deliberately stirring up tensions which culminated in Thursday's killing of at least four Palestinians in the West Bank village of Nahhalin.

"For five or six days before the killings, Israeli border guards had been systematically provoking the villagers by making religious and personal insults", an ICRC spokesman, Mr Carlos Bauverd, said.

During the pre-dawn Israeli raid on Nahhalin, part of which was witnessed by the ICRC, Israeli soldiers opened fire "without discrimination and without restraint" he said. . . . Apart from the Nahhalin killings, the ICRC condemned Israel for an "increasingly frequent use of firearms and acts of physical violence against defenceless civilians".

Mr Bauverd said that among recent violations of the Fourth Geneva Convention had been systematic violence against medical teams and ambulance drivers who were employed by the Red Cross and by the UN Works and Relief Agency for Palestinian Refugees.

"These people have been pulled from their vehicles and beaten by Israeli soldiers. When drivers have tried to dismantle roadblocks to get to wounded people they have been arrested". . . .

Singled out for particular criticism was Israel's policy of deporting Palestinian activists to Lebanon, something which is outlawed under Article 49, collective punishments and the destruction of houses, and excessive violence against demonstrators.
Guardian 15th April 1989

The role of the paramilitary Border Police in one of the bloodiest single incidents of the uprising has brought more unwelcome attention to a force that has often attracted controversy since it was founded as a professional frontier guard in 1953.

Until the *intifada* erupted in December 1987, its green-bereted men — known by their Hebrew acronym as Magavniks — had carried out most of the routine security duties in the West Bank . . .

The Border Police, which answers to the Ministry of Police rather than Defence, is a 5,500-strong regular force, although many of its lower ranks arrive after being rejected even as cooks or drivers by the army. Many hold extreme rightwing political views. . . .

The force has a tendency to be so brutal as to simply terrify Palestinians into submission, although — and this makes Nahhalin unusual — that toughness is not necessarily a problem of being trigger-happy.

They are widely accused of sexual abuse and there have been some allegations of rape. Many people from Nahhalin said on Thursday that tension had been mounting after Border Police began to make obscene remarks or gestures at local women.
Guardian 15th April 1989

Jewish settlers in the occupied West Bank yesterday wounded three Arabs when they shot up a village near Ramallah after Israeli vehicles had been attacked by stone-throwers.

A few hours earlier, settlers fired at Arab houses in the West Bank city of Hebron after petrol bombs were thrown at an Israeli car. It was not known whether anyone was hurt in this shooting.

Highlighting their anger, a group of settlers also appealed to the rightwing minister, Mr Ariel Sharon, to allow them a free hand for revenge against the stone-throwers. "Arik, do something. You can break the *intifada* like you broke Gaza", a settler said, referring to the former general's successful campaign in the occupied Gaza Strip in the early 1970s.

"You're right. I know what should be done but I'm a voice in the wilderness in the Cabinet and nothing will happen unless you press (Prime Minister) Shamir to let me handle things", the minister said.

"What should be done is to put all the Arabs on a skewer and roast them", a passing motorist shouted. "Throw the Arabs out", shouted a young woman.
Guardian 27th May 1989

. . . "The West Bank is different from the Gaza strip in three or four ways. The West Bank is five times the area; the Gaza strip can easily be sealed off. Over 60 per cent of the residents of the Gaza strip live in refugees camps, against 10 per cent on the West Bank. And there are the settlers." Some 70,000 Jewish settlers, many of them highly critical of what they see as General Mitzna's soft approach, live among 850,000 Palestinians on the West Bank, against only 2,000 among the 650,000 inhabitants of the Gaza strip.
Independent June 1989

Ariel Sharon . . . Likud Hawk . . . told reporters in the Golan Heights, wrested from Syria in the 1967 war and held onto in the 1973 war, that "we are in a war. It's a different kind of war. But it's a war. In order to be able to overcome all our problems . . . the most important thing is to restore law and order, to bring to an end terror and violence, called here *intifada*, and to eliminate the heads of the terrorist organisations and first of all Arafat."

Mr Sharon, now Trade and Industry Minister, has made such threats before, and Israel is not above assassination. As defence minister, Mr Sharon launched Israel's invasion of Lebanon in 1982, with the declared aim of clearing 'Fatahland' from south Lebanon. . . .
Independent 18th July 1989

At the village of Artas, near Bethlehem, the army yesterday morning destroyed the houses of five men whom they said were members of a Palestinian "shock troop" who had murdered a collaborator.
Independent 5th May 1989

At least 140 Palestinians were wounded and three people were killed in the Gaza Strip . . . hospital sources said, in the highest daily casualty toll since the uprising began 18 months ago. . . .

While the chief Israeli army spokesman, Brigadier-General Ephraim

Lapid, said 77 people were taken to hospital, Gaza Strip hospitals reported treating twice as many victims.

However, the UN Relief and Works Agency in Gaza said 400 Arabs were injured by gunfire, beatings or teargas inhalation on Saturday.

Arab hospitals in Gaza said troops shot and wounded eight people in continuing protests yesterday.

The violence occurred during the Muslim holiday of Id al-Fitr, which is marked by prayers and visits to the grave of relatives. Gen Lapid said residents of Nuseirat refugee camp provoked the most serious violence. . . . helicopter dropped teargas canisters and troop reinforcements were called in. In the clash, two people were shot dead and at least 42 people, including two Israeli soldiers were wounded.

Guardian 8th May 1989

. . . Mr Shamir said in Tel Aviv that no effort would be spared to catch the murderers of Steven Rosenfeld, a 48-year-old American immigrant, found stabbed to death . . . near an Arab village adjoining the West Bank settlement of Ariel.

He was the 21st Israeli to be killed during the *intifada*. About 520 Palestinians have been killed. . . .

"Israel's security forces will uproot this violence with an iron fist" Mr Shamir said. . . .

Ariel, with a population of 6,000, attracted controversy recently when it ordered Palestinians employed there to wear tags saying 'foreign worker'. . . .

Guardian 25th June 1989

In chilling proof that the Israeli Army has learned nothing in the 17 months since the *intifada* began, three Palestinians were killed and more than 140 injured in the Gaza strip over the weekend, while one soldier suffered a broken jaw. . . .

A second depressing aspect of the latest events is that the Israelis are still using lethal force against youngsters with stones and slingshots — a seven-month-old girl was among those hit by bullets.

Most depressing of all is that with 466 Palestinians dead, in spite of the renunciation of violence by the PLO and its recognition of Israel's right to exist within secure borders, a change of administration in Washington and a more moderate line from Mr Gorbachev's Moscow, peace in the Middle East is as distant as ever.

The Independent 8th May 1989

The Israeli Prime Minister, Mr Yitzhak Shamir, said yesterday that proposals for Palestinian elections in the occupied territories were more public relations than substance, reinforcing Arab accusations that the initiative was aimed at ending the *intifada* without conceding real political power to the Palestinians.

He told a parliamentary committee that those elected would not form a parliament: "The elections have more importance from a public relations point of view than in a practical sense."
Guardian 27th June 1989

As well as joining the kidnappers in the Lebanon the Israelis have been extending their territory there too. The *Independent* reported on the 25th April:

While world attention has been focused on the crisis afflicting Beirut and central Lebanon, Israel has been quietly extending its hold on areas in the south within its self-declared security zone.

At the weekend, 300 farmers were evicted from their land just over the border from Israel. About 40 square miles of Lebanese territory were effectively annexed by the Israeli forces, according to Lebanese sources. It was the second instance this year of Lebanese citizens being expelled from their property in the south.

In January, dozens of people were evicted from the Israeli-occupied town of Chebaa, on the eastern slopes of Mount Hermon, the snow-covered mountain ridge which forms the south-eastern frontier between Israeli-occupied south Lebanon and Syria. It is at Chebaa that the 300 farmers have now arrived, together with what flocks and other possessions they were able to take with them. Having received no compensation for their lost land, they are now penniless and homeless.

Eight Palestinians, described by Israel as leaders of the uprising in the occupied territories, were deported to Lebanon yesterday, as the army went on alert to guard Jewish settlers planning mass marches in the West Bank today.

The eight deportees, who were detained last August, included representatives of the mainstream Fatah movement and the leftwing Democratic Front for the Liberation of Palestine. All had lost their appeals to the High Court.

They were taken by helicopter to the Zumraya crossing point at the northern edge of Israel's 'security zone' in southern Lebanon and ordered to cross into Syrian-controlled territory.

The latest expulsions came as the authorities are seeking to streamline the process of deportation and increase the maximum single period of detention without trial from six months to a year. . . .

The Shin Bet security service, meanwhile, was congratulating itself over Wednesday's killing in Gaza of Muhamad Abu Nasser. . . . [He] was shot down in a taxi in what appeared to have been a pre-planned ambush. . . .
Guardian 30th June 1989

In perhaps the most ominous development, the home in Jerusalem of a left-wing Knesset member, Dedi Zucker, was attacked. Mr Zucker, of the

Citizens' Rights Movement, and an outspoken critic of Israeli army excesses in the occupied territories, said youths involved in the attack shouted "Death to Arabs, death to Zucker". . . .

The attack on Mr Zucker's house together with the jostling of the Labour Party leader, Shimon Peres, at the funeral of one of the victims on Friday, has had the leader writers railing against what *Maariv* calls "the terrible deterioration of Israeli society". For *The Jerusalem Post* "Jews, the victims of racist prejudice throughout the ages, are now committing the worst kind of racism themselves and are meting out collective punishment. The spectre of hatred is raging throughout the land, while passive bystanders allow the outrages to take place."

The fears of *Maariv*'s editorial writer that "the civil war is almost here" may seem hopelessly exaggerated. But passions are high, and Meir Kahane, the leader of the overtly racist Kach movement, has little difficulty in tapping an underlying current of extremist feeling.

The Independent 10th July 1989

"The [peace] initiative does not rule out the suppression of the *intifada*. We extend one hand for peace, and have the other hand free to strike at the rioters", Mr Shamir said. Any hopes that he might show more flexibility on what the initiative terms the permanent settlement of Judea, Samaria (the West Bank) and Gaza were equally dashed. He ruled out the main Palestinian demands: an Israeli withdrawal and the establishment of a Palestinian state. "A Palestinian state will not arise and will not be." Invoking an Old Testament oath, he declared: "Whoever says it — may his tongue cleave to the roof of his mouth". Later to the Knesset itself, he spelled out his adamantine opposition to trading any land for peace, thereby ensuring the near impossibility of any Arab side even discussing the proposal: "We will not give the Arabs a single centimetre. We will not give them anything. That is it."

The Independent 18th May 1989

The defence establishment has already started implementing what Shmuel Goren, Co-ordinator for Activities for the occupied territories, called a fundamental change in policy, to give the Palestinians a foretaste of the repressive measures they can expect if they reject Israeli election proposals. Tens of thousands of Gazans have been ordered to pack up their jobs on construction sites and in restaurants in Israel proper. Mr Goren said permits for Gazans to work in Israel will only be given in future for legitimate reasons. And he said the next step would be formulating a comprehensive policy towards the West Bank and Gaza strip.

Last month one Likud minister proposed sealing the territories off from Israel as a punitive measure. This would deprive many families of their livelihoods, particularly in Gaza, where there is little work. However the proposal was rejected by the chief of general staff, Dan Shomron. "We

should not bring the Arabs to the point where they have nothing to lose", he told the Knesset foreign affairs and defence committee.
The Independent 18th May 1989

In the Gaza strip, men and women with computer terminals and Polaroid cameras began the lengthy process of issuing yet another identity card to Palestinian residents to increase the scrutiny and supervision of those hoping to work in Israel proper.

Gaza itself was at a standstill, brought to a halt by two competing agents of control: the underground leadership of the *intifada* had called for days of strikes to mark the anniversary of the 1967 defeat, and the Israeli army had placed the 650,000 people of Gaza under indefinite 24-hour curfew.
. . .

The flash new cards bore magnetic strips, like credit cards. The information stored on these, a military spokesman explained, would help control employment in Israel proper. Despite the *intifada* . . . neither Israeli employers nor Palestinian workers have managed to disengage themselves economically. Tens of thousands of Gazans continue to work in Israel, doing the jobs that no self-respecting Jew will do, washing dishes, humping cement, or clearing garbage. Those with prison records or who have served in administrative detention (internment) will not get the new cards.
The Independent 3rd June 1989

Four young soldiers were acquitted yesterday by a military court of the manslaughter of a 42-year old Palestinian beaten to death after trying to protect his son from arrest. They were convicted of the lesser charge of brutality. The judges advocate agreed with the accused that the victim died not from the beating at his house but from wounds suffered later when he was held at an army outpost. They concluded that the culprits would never be found among the 20 or so other soldiers who participated in the beating.

This was the first trial of soldiers accused of beating to death a Palestinian in their charge since the beginning of the uprising . . .

During the trial earlier this year, soldier after soldier testified about systematic brutality in an atmosphere of fear and racial loathing . . .

Dedi Zucker, Knesset member for the left-wing Citizens' Rights Movement, called the verdict 'the most important since the beginning of the *Intifada*'. He said it was the first time a court had questioned the army's policy.

Prosecutions and disciplinary actions have been rare; the army protects its own. Two weeks ago, an Israeli colonel escaped with dismissal for ordering soldiers to break the arms and legs of Palestinians already arrested.

Since the uprising began in December 1987, two soldiers have been convicted of manslaughter. Nearly 500 Palestinians have been shot dead or beaten to death in this period.
The Independent 26th May 1989

5

The Uprising of Youth: The *Intifada*

It is exciting, sometimes frightening, to witness as an outsider the birth of any new movement, to watch it from its unco-ordinated, hesitant start, gather confidence, momentum, purpose and appeal until it reaches a stage of worldwide recognition.

I was in a privileged position, as the then senior United Nations official in the Israeli-occupied Gaza strip, to observe the genesis of the *intifada* as a movement, from its schoolyard origins in the Gazan city of Rafah in October 1986 until the time it successfully challenged long-established attitudes and positions on the core problem of the Middle East — the Israeli/Palestinian dispute.

The *intifada*, or the 'shakening' in its English translation, has indeed shaken the log-jam of Middle East politics and conceptions. First, it has considerably eroded the traditional Western support for Israel on which that state's future ultimately depends. It has induced an even-handed Western appreciation of the need to solve, justly and urgently, the long-unresolved problem of the Palestinian people.

Second, it has shaken the hitherto uncritical support by world Jewry for the Israeli government's hard-line attitudes in its relations with the Palestinians. Third, it has enabled the Palestine Liberation Organisation to make radical changes in its policies and now to pursue actively the path of peaceful territorial compromise with Israel over the land of Palestine. Finally, it has forced increasing numbers of Israelis to realise that the pre-*intifada* status of occupied lands and subject peoples can never be returned to, and that the days of Palestinians playing the role of Helots to an Israeli Sparta are over. The Palestinians are now for the Israelis an entity, a people to be reckoned with . . .

World leaders who wish to help should be clear as to the *raison d'être* of the *intifada*. It is a movement started by the generation born or brought up under Israeli occupation, knowing no other form of rule. Young people

103

disillusioned by the lack of real interest in the world in solving the Palestinian problem; the charade of American shuttle diplomacy; the Jordanian
option, which was no option in their opinion; the failure of the UN and
the Arab League to project their case, and of the PLO to achieve anything
for them; even their parents and community leaders for having accepted
so docilely the humiliation of the status quo of occupation for so long.
Young people sensing the contempt the average Israeli felt for all things
Palestinian, the indignity of seeing their fathers go smiling, cap in hand,
to an Israeli official to seek approval for almost any activity, domestic or
business.

It was the young who sensed correctly that if they wanted to be free of
Israeli rule, they must achieve it by themselves. It was the young who
decided to take to the streets to show the world their contempt for Israeli
rule. It was the young who agreed to defy death, maiming, beating and
imprisonment to continue their campaign, who knew that for them a hero's
death was better than a life of slavery. It was they who breathed life and
self-respect again into their elders and led the whole community into the
intifada.

The young, in the course of action they chose, were certainly not the
dupes and pawns of the PLO; indeed the PLO was taken almost as much
by surprise as the Israelis at the onset of the *intifada*. While the *intifada*
has entrusted the PLO with the negotiations, it is my opinion that the
parameters are clearly laid down. They want the Israelis out of the West
Bank and Gaza, but they want to live in peace with them. They will not
accept autonomy under Israeli auspices because the young will not endorse
it. They will not accept — as the Israelis might want — negotiations
through traditional Palestinian dignitaries in the territories, because again
the young will not agree to it. They will not accept elections under Israeli
auspices, because they distrust the process and believe the candidates
putting themselves forward are placing themselves at risk of incarceration
in Israeli detention camps or deportation.

They will not accept any scaling down of the *intifada*, unless it is accom-
panied by copper-bottomed guarantees that their objectives will be realised, for they know that the continuance of the *intifada*, however painful,
does much more harm to Israel.

I believe these are the realities which must be taken into consideration
by any country seeking to bring about an end to the Israeli/Palestinian
dispute. The *intifada* has given the best possible opportunity for a secure,
prosperous and peaceful future for both Israelis and Palestinians, living
side by side in their own lands as neighbours, trading partners and future
friends. It should not be missed.

The Independent   BERNARD MILES
13th April 1989